INVERCLYDE LIBRARIES

PORT GLASGOW

19 AUG 2013	17 OCT	10 JAN
	GOUROCK	7|5
5/16 McFARLANE		

WITHDRAWN

INVERCLYDE LIBRARIES

This book is to be returned on or before
the last date above. It may be borrowed for
a further period if not in demand.

For enquiries and renewals Tel: (01475) 712323

GW00771092

THE UNKNOWN PETER CUSHING

MICHAEL G. McGLASSON

BearManor
Media

Albany, Georgia

The Unknown Peter Cushing
© 2011 Michael G. McGlasson. All rights reserved.

All rights reserved. No portion of this publication may be reproduced, stored, and/or copied electronically (except for academic use as a source), nor transmitted in any form or by any means without the prior written permission of the publisher and/or the author.

Published in the USA by:
BearManor Media
PO Box 1129
Duncan, OK 73534-1129
www.BearManorMedia.com

ISBN: 1-59393-665-6
ISBN-13: 978-1-59393-665-5

Printed in the United States.

Design and Layout by Allan T. Duffin.

Table of Contents

Dedication

To Rebecca Lorraine Reid

1954-1994

Death is here and death is there,
Death is busy everywhere,
All around, within, beneath,
Above is death—and we are death.
Death has set his mark and seal
On all we are and all we feel,
On all we know and all we fear,
First our pleasures die—and then
Our hopes, and then our fears—and when
These are dead, the debt is due,
Dust claims dust—and we die too.
All things that we love and cherish,
Like ourselves must fade and perish;
Such is our rude mortal lot—
Love itself would, did they not.

—*Percy Bysshe Shelley*

Acknowledgments

I would like to thank the following individuals and institutions for their invaluable assistance in the writing of *The Unknown Peter Cushing*: The Newspaper Library, British Library; *The Stage* and *The Era* online databases; Andrew Kirk, curatorial assistant, the Theatre Museum; Mary M. Huth, Rush Rhees Library, University of Rochester, Rochester, New York; the Porter Library, Special Collections, University of Waterloo, Ontario, Canada; Christopher Gullo, for permission to use excerpts from his biography on Peter Cushing and for providing some great photos; Michael Kilgarriff, the Irving Society, London; Warren R. Cushing, genealogist and Cushing family researcher; David Stuckey, compiler of *Card Times: The Cushing Collection*; David Cushing, for the Cushing family coat-of-arms; the online John Johnson Collection of Printed Ephemera; Joyce Condon, information officer of the Royal Institute of Chartered Surveyors, London; Diane Clements, director of the Library and Museum of Freemasonry, London; Georgianna Ziegler, head of reference, Folger Shakespeare Library, Washington, D.C.; Barbara Shelley; Dan Dorman; Kristi McNulty, assistant librarian for local history, Fremantle City Library, Fremantle, Australia; and of course, Peter Wilton Cushing, O.B.E. ***In Pace Requiescat***.

§

Introduction

In his preface to *The Picture of Dorian Gray*, Oscar Wilde declares "Those who go beneath the surface do so at their own peril." What exactly does Wilde mean by this? I believe he is offering a warning to those who are not satisfied with what appears to be reality and wish to go deeper to uncover forbidden knowledge. As a writer, Oscar Wilde often broke away from his own warning so he could explore the human subconscious mind where the true nature of man surely lies, dormant and inexplicable. Wilde also knew that when a writer attempts to penetrate the unknown, that which lies hidden might turn out to be something completely unexpected, perhaps even dangerous like Dorian Gray's fatal portrait or Dr. Jekyll's evil doppelganger twin Mr. Hyde.

However, Wilde is not suggesting that a writer should leave the unknown alone but must approach it with caution and foresight. Personally, I am convinced that the human imagination is the key that fits the rusted lock of what Poe calls the "Plutonian shore" and allows that strange door to be opened. In the 1939 film version of Arthur Conan Doyle's *The Hound of the Baskervilles*, Basil Rathbone as Sherlock Holmes makes the astonishing announcement that "If we go beyond the facts, use our imaginations . . . imagine what might have happened, then act upon it, we usually find ourselves justified."

My first encounter with Peter Cushing occurred while sitting in front of an old RCA black and white TV, the kind with two big plastic knobs, one for volume, and the other as a channel selector. The movie on the TV screen was Stanley Kubrick's version of Vladimir Nabokov's *Lolita* (1962) with James Mason as the rascally decadent Humbert Humbert, Shelley Winters as the sex-starved Charlotte Haze, and Sue Lyon as the beautiful nymphet Lolita. Although I was not familiar with Nabokov's novel and had no interest in watching an old man attempt to seduce a thirteen year-old girl, James Mason caught my eye, due to starring in one of my favorite films of the late 1950s, *Journey to the Center of the Earth*, based on the novel by Jules Verne in which Professor Lindenbrook (Mason) and his comrade Alex McKuen (Pat Boone) journey to Iceland to penetrate unknown worlds beneath the earth.

In one scene, Humbert, Charlotte, and Lolita are jammed in the front seat of a car at the drive-in and are watching a very strange movie. One of the characters in this movie is extremely upset over something, for he suddenly rips a handful of bandages from his face as a very shocked, elegant-looking young man dressed in a blood-stained coat looks on. This young man was, of course, Peter Cushing, and the movie was *The Curse of Frankenstein*, released in 1957 by Hammer. To this very day, I often wonder why Kubrick inserted this particular Hammer shot into *Lolita*, but it may be a sort of metaphor, a well-disguised hint that the beautiful Lolita is a monster and that Humbert, much like Baron Victor Frankenstein, will pay dearly for his deranged curiosity.

Several years later, I had the opportunity to see *The Curse of Frankenstein* on the big screen at (ironically) a local drive-in.

This film, the first of Hammer's technicolor horror masterpieces, certainly lived up to my expectations, for I remember being completely overwhelmed by Cushing's portrayal of Baron Frankenstein, the quintessential mad scientist whose obsession with death and dying culminates in a date with the guillotine. In character, Cushing is utterly devoted to his scientific goals and has no qualms about possible dangers related to his "project" to reanimate the dead, in this instance, a body stolen from the gallows with the hands of a sculptor and the brain of poor old Professor Bernstein, pushed to his death from a balcony by the Baron. In essence, Cushing's character is much like the literary Victor in Mary Shelley's masterpiece *Frankenstein; Or, the Modern Prometheus*, a young and highly ambitious scientist seeking forbidden knowledge which he acquires upon opening that strange door to the unknown.

After that serendipitous day at the drive-in, my interest in the life of Peter Cushing slowly expanded until sometime in early 2004, Christopher Gullo, proprietor of the web-based Peter Cushing Museum and Association and the Peter Cushing Association on Facebook, contacted me with the news that he was planning on writing a biography on the "Gentle Man of Horror" and that he wanted his manuscript to be edited from beginning to end. At first, I was somewhat apprehensive about taking on such a dense project (400-plus pages), but after reviewing what Gullo had written, I decided to give it a try.

As I progressed through the manuscript, my interest in Cushing was transformed into one of fascination, due to discovering many new and surprising aspects about his private life and his career as an actor that I previously did not know. By the strangest coincidence, I was already involved in researching the life of Peter's paternal grandfather Henry William Cushing who once "tread the boards" with the great Sir Henry Irving at the Lyceum Theatre as a secondary character actor.

When Gullo learned of what I was doing, he was astonished at the information I had uncovered concerning Henry Cushing and suggested that I insert some of it into the first chapter of his book; in fact, his astonishment was so great that he agreed to write a foreword to *All In the Blood: The Theatrical Ancestry of Peter Cushing*, published as an Ebook in 2006. However, after finding more information on Henry Cushing related to his acting (and operatic) careers, I quickly decided to revamp the entire manuscript of *All In the Blood* to create something unique, a sort of creative, non-fiction extrapolation on not only Henry Cushing but also his famous grandson. But after giving it much thought, I came to the conclusion that my material might be too esoteric and would not appeal to a broad range of readers. So, in order to be less esoteric, I decided to make Peter Cushing the main focus of the book but still retain the material I had collected over the years on Henry Cushing who admittedly is not a well-recognized British thespian.

After making this decision, I began to consider if such a project had any worth or value, especially for Peter's numerous fans and admirers on both sides of the Atlantic. Admittedly, I was not at all interested in rehashing what was already "common knowledge" about Peter Cushing related to his life as a professional actor. Therefore, if the project was to have any value, I would have to focus on areas that other biographers have somehow failed to discuss. Then, much like an epiphany, I realized that the life of Henry Cushing and that of his famous grandson were so interconnected that they could not be separated, especially in relation to their shared acting legacy.

There are currently a number of books that cover Peter Cushing's acting career on the stage, the movie screen, and television. For example, there is David Miller's *The Peter Cushing Companion* (Reynolds & Hearn, 2000), considered by many Cushing fans as the definitive guide to his stage and screen career, and Tony Earnshaw's *An Actor and a Rare One: Peter Cushing as Sherlock Holmes* (Scarecrow Press, 2001) which discusses Cushing's career from his early days in regional theatre to his role as Conan Doyle's great detective, aided by anecdotes and reminiscences by colleagues and Cushing himself.

There is also *Peter Cushing: The Gentle Man of Horror and His 91 Films* (McFarland, 1992) by Deborah Del Vecchio and Tom Johnson which offers "A Profile of Peter Cushing," a scant ten pages in length and heavy with redundancies related to Cushing's acting career. And then there is *In All Sincerity . . . Peter Cushing* (Xlibris, 2004) by Christopher Gullo, perhaps the most devoted Cushing fan the world has ever known. Standing at 407 pages, this book is ponderous with much of the same "common knowledge" on Cushing's acting career covering a fifty-year period. Biographically, *In All Sincerity* does not fully explore the intricacies of Cushing's life with the exception of Chapter One ("A Star is Born, 1913-1939"), a mere nineteen pages in length. From this point on, *In All Sincerity* contains material almost identical to that found in similar books; however, it does offer many insightful interviews that adds to its attractiveness and value as a worthy addition to Cushing bibliography.

Not surprisingly, the best source for biographical information on Peter Cushing is his autobiography, published by Weidenfeld and Nicolson in 1986 when Peter was seventy-three years old. In this "memoir" as he refers to it, Peter offers to the reader his life story, beginning with his birth and childhood and ending in 1971 with the death of his beloved wife Helen. Like most autobiographies, it does contain a great amount of exposition and offers a fleeting glimpse into Cushing's private affairs related to love and loss, failure, success, disappointment, and personal tragedy.

In my own humble opinion, the most fascinating aspect of Peter's autobiography concerns his family's past which is covered in "Myself When Young" from page nine to thirteen. Here, Peter divulges some of the facts (and possible fallacies) concerning his acting legacy by briefly discussing the major "players"—his aunt Maude Ashton, his step-uncle Wilton Herriot, the mysterious uncle Bertie, and most importantly, Henry William Cushing, his paternal grandfather who was once a member of Sir Henry Irving's acting company at the famous Lyceum Theatre between 1887 and 1897. For some strange reason, Peter teases the reader by only revealing basic information on Henry Cushing and his career on the stage. My first reaction to all of this was in the form of a question—was this all that Peter really knew about his grandfather and his other acting relatives?

After conducting years of research on Peter's acting legacy, it now appears that he was ignorant of the full story, one that has remained in the dark for more than one hundred and twenty years. In essence, there are many more fascinating facts and circumstances related to the lives of his acting ancestors than anyone has ever suspected. For instance, Peter relates that the truth concerning poor uncle Bertie was "a skeleton in the cupboard;" however, after years of attempting to uncover additional information, I have succeeded in revealing more skeletons lying within the same cupboard, rattling together amid the accumulated dust and debris.

Of all the individuals contacted over the course of six years regarding my research on Peter's ancestral past, only two offered high-quality comments on what I had uncovered. The first was Christopher Gullo who kindly supplied the following observations:

Since the time of his death in 1994, much has been written about British actor Peter Cushing, best known for his horror and fantasy films with Hammer during the 1950s and through the 1970s. Several biographies on this cult character actor have been published and Cushing himself even wrote two autobiographies during the 1980s, but *The Unknown Peter Cushing* has accomplished the seemingly impossible by revealing information about Cushing's ancestors that has never seen the light of day. For those who believe in destiny or some higher power, *The Unknown Peter Cushing* demonstrates a unique connection between Peter Cushing and his grandfather Henry William Cushing who appeared on the stage of the Lyceum Theatre with the famed Sir Henry Irving in numerous productions of *Faust* which some say served as the inspiration for the character of Count Dracula. Thus, Mr. McGlasson's book is truly a remarkable feat of sleuthing, worthy of another character played by Peter—the great Sherlock Holmes—considering that Cushing himself was apparently unable to uncover as much information for his autobiographies. Determined to delve even deeper into Peter's ancestral past, Mr. McGlasson continued his quest and not long after obtained a copy of Henry Cushing's obituary as well as additional playbills listing him among the cast lists. Initially, I thought this new information would *surely* be the last remaining documentation one could turn up, but he proved me wrong and traced the family lineage back to the fifteenth century in England. And to my profound amazement, he also discovered that another Cushing descendant was an actor in the early 1700s, the acting gene being firmly implanted in the Cushing DNA by one John Cushing. Without a doubt, *The Unknown Peter Cushing* offers a meticulously researched look into the ancestry of Peter Cushing and his theatrical roots, and if you happen to be a fan of the "Gentle Man of Horror" or are just generally interested in British theatre, then I believe you will be well-rewarded for your curiosity. Mr. McGlasson has done the acting world a service by revealing some of its previously unwritten past, and personally, I am most glad that he did.

The second was Dan Dorman, an avid collector of Cushing memorabilia and the proprietor of the *Cinema is Dead* film review blogspot. His comments on *The Unknown Peter Cushing* were provided in November of 2010:

To an extent, Peter Cushing has become something of a mentor to the countless fans who find themselves addicted to the actor's life and work. Say what you will, but it is an addiction, for what compels a person to watch Hammer's *Dracula* one hundred and fifty-three times and never cease to be amazed at Cushing's stoic entrance or his simple mannerisms, like in the way he carefully and knowingly draws blood from Michael Gough and injects it into Melissa Stribling? These are not the marks of a mere performer; these are indeed the trappings of an ingenious mind and an immortal artist, one who leaves you holding your breath until their next slightest move or briefest line. Cushing's life was destined to be dedicated to his craft, and all great actors somehow enlighten us and are capable of revealing facets of ourselves that perhaps we do not always prefer to see. They can teach us to be better people too because Peter Cushing taught us not only through the art of performance but also through his spirit. How many countless pupils has his gentlemanly legacy taught the proper way to handle oneself amid disorder and chaos or to take the time to enjoy the most uncomplicated things life has to offer, like enjoying birds from your window, or knowing when to be courteous and compassionate to all living things? Peter Cushing's own answer to the latter question would be easy—always. These are not the lessons of an ordinary teacher. Anyone with even the slightest bit of interest in Peter Cushing the human being will tell you right away that he was so much more than what is normally required from an average person. It may sound pious in a way, but he never failed to give back to his fans (his extended family) despite whatever he was feeling or experiencing at any given moment, even in the worst of health. He would never hesitate to make that special connection to anyone, anywhere, anytime. Sadly, I missed my chance to make my own personal connection with him, for by the time I was ready to reach out he had already shuffled off this mortal coil. I have been fortunate, as is most every fan (whether they are aware of it or not) to belong to an extended family of friends the whole world over, for every Peter Cushing fan is a member of his family. And like all families, there may be relatives that you only get to see or hear from on rare occasions (and some you may never have a chance to meet at all), but we all share the same unmistakable familial bond or as Van Helsing might have put it, the same blood. *The Unknown Peter Cushing* provides several new aspects on this great actor that have never been revealed in such extraordinary depth before, a legacy of which perhaps even Peter himself was not fully aware. Through the tireless and captivating work of Mr. McGlasson, we have been drawn a little closer to the roots of the man we have all come to know through countless stage, television and film appearances. If there are still beginners amongst you earnest and intrepid readers, rest assured that you are in good company because no matter where you go, no matter what the hour, you are certainly never alone.

At this point, I would like to make it perfectly clear that a good percentage of what is discussed in the text is currently "unknown," or in other words, is not "common knowledge" for most readers with the possible exception of a handful of Peter's zealous fans scattered across the globe. This is especially relevant to the first and second chapters, "Rogues, Vagabonds, and Scoundrels" and "The Life and Times of Henry William Cushing." The third and fourth chapters, however, do contain "known" facts on Peter Cushing, but because of my desire to cover more ephemeral and esoteric circumstances, what is known and what is unknown often overlaps.

In addition, I should point out that the chapters on Peter ("The Moon in June is Full of Beauty") and his wife Helen ("Helen: The Poetry of Her Presence") do not cover everything that occurred in their lives like a standard biography. Therefore, the primary focus of *The Unknown Peter Cushing* is on Peter and his familial acting ancestry, his artistic tendencies, his stage acting, and how when Helen Beck entered the picture, Peter's life changed forever.

I would also like to share my disappointment for being unable to locate a photograph of Henry William Cushing. Before beginning to write this book, I was hoping that I might be able to locate the "daguerreotype" (actually a tintype) of Henry Cushing mentioned by Peter in his 1986 autobiographical memoir, but unfortunately, this did not happen. Peter's former secretary Joyce Broughton was unable to furnish any information on the whereabouts of this photograph which I assume after being sold to the highest bidder is now in private hands somewhere in England.

****

On the morning of August 11, 1994, Peter Wilton Cushing entered the misty regions of the Unknown at the age of eighty-one after battling prostate cancer for more than twenty years. The hospice in which he died quietly and peacefully is located in the city of

Canterbury, the birthplace of the great English poet and playwright Christopher Marlowe, perhaps best known for *The Tragical History of Doctor Faustus*, a tale concerning an aging scholar who wishes to possess ultimate knowledge, the forbidden fruit of life and death, and agrees to sell his immortal soul to Mephistopheles, Satan's dark angel, in exchange for such knowledge. Unfortunately, Dr. Faustus meets a very bad end with his life and reputation utterly destroyed, much like Victor Frankenstein, the obsessed "mad scientist" who dared to emulate God as the reanimator of the dead.

Without a doubt, Peter Cushing was the quintessential screen villain and hero of horror cinema, due to his remarkable ability to express an entire range of human emotions while in character. But off-screen, Peter Cushing was one of the kindest and most compassionate human beings to ever walk the earth, at least in the opinion of the numerous actors and actresses that worked with him over a span of some fifty years. He was also completely devoted to his wife Helen, born Violet Helene Beck in 1905 in St. Petersburg, Russia, and likewise, she was utterly devoted to him, for in a letter discovered by Peter after her death, Helen writes "Do not pine for me, my beloved Peter . . . and remember we will meet again when the time is right. This is my promise." [1] From these words, it is beyond any doubt that Peter loved, if not adored, his Helen with unbounded passion, much like Kharis, the high priest of Hammer's *The Mummy* whose ancient heart was filled with tenderness for the beautiful Princess Ananka.

After Cushing's death, the outpouring of sadness from his fans and former co-stars was great, for they knew that someone of his caliber was not going to re-appear anytime soon. Hammer actress Barbara Shelley recalls that Peter "was a very special man, and a fine and generous actor. My memories of knowing and acting with him are among the happiest of my career." [2] Friend and colleague Christopher Lee adds that Peter "was the gentlest and most generous of men," and that it "could be said of him that he died because he was too good for this world." [3] Hammer actress Hazel Court relates that "I have never heard anyone say anything bad about Peter . . . He was a remarkable person and I always felt, though he was born in the twentieth century, that he really belonged in the eighteenth century." [4] But what was unknown to most of his fans, admirers, and even close friends was that Peter Cushing's death symbolized the culmination of a long acting legacy dating back to the days when actors were considered as nothing more than "rogues and vagabonds" living outside of traditional British society as non-conformists.

As demonstrated in his autobiography, Peter was fascinated with the acting career of his paternal grandfather Henry William Cushing (1842-1899), a member of Sir Henry Irving's Lyceum troupe of performers who shared the stage with such notables as Ellen Terry, Gordon Craig (Terry's son), Sir Johnston Forbes-Robertson, John Martin Harvey, and the doomed William Terriss. As the story goes, Peter's aunt Maude Ashton (her stage name), his father's actress sister, presented him with some "beautiful souvenir programs" of Sir Henry's productions at the Lyceum Theatre. One of these programs was for the historical play *King Henry VIII* and "sandwiched between Mr. Reynolds . . . and Miss Ellen Terry, was Mr. Cushing." [5] Peter then recounts a portrait of Henry Cushing gazing down from a shrouded parlor wall. In his eyes, this portrait of his grandfather with the "formidable face of a disciplinarian" [6] was an icon deserving of much awe and respect, especially after realizing that Henry Cushing had "tread the boards" alongside Sir Henry, the "First Knight" of the Victorian stage. Perhaps at this time, Peter made the momentous decision to become an actor as a way of emulating his grandfather and to continue on with his familial acting legacy.

As might be expected, Peter started in on his father with questions about his family acting roots, but George Cushing, "a most reserved and uncommunicative soul," refused to disclose what Peter wished to know. Yet through some "inquisitive probing," [7] Peter's father did relent with a few shadowy details. Exactly why George Cushing was so reluctant to tell his curious son about the theatrical exploits of his father Henry Cushing and other aspects of the family acting past remains somewhat unclear, yet it may have had much to do with the fact that George Cushing was a Freemason, as was Henry Cushing.

But since Peter's father was born during the height of the reign of Queen Victoria in 1881, "doing the right thing" [8] and only revealing what was proper and forthright to a young child was of prime importance. If this is accurate, then it is not surprising that George Cushing's initial reaction to Peter's revelation that he wanted to become an actor was one of astonishment and dismay. "It has always puzzled me," writes Peter, "why he was so averse to my continuing the tradition. Perhaps he still regarded it as full of rogues and vagabonds, beset with hordes of loose women," [9] also known as actresses.

However, Peter's aunt Maude appears to have been of the other persuasion, for she was willing to tell Peter whatever he wished to know and had no scruples about being "proper and forthright." In fact, aunt Maude was so straightforward that she once remarked to her young nephew, "My deah, I'm surprised you didn't become another Oscar Wilde, perhaps not in the poetic sense, but most certainly in the other, treated as you were from the cradle as a gel," [10] a reference to Peter's mother dressing him up as a girl and Wilde's alleged preference for the male of the species.

Sometime before the publication of his autobiography, Peter stumbled upon a collection of birth, marriage, and death certificates, and almost immediately noticed "some discrepancy regarding Grand-dad's rank and profession," [11] particularly about being a quantity surveyor, a type of engineer responsible for determining the amount and cost of materials needed to construct a building. These discrepancies went directly against what little information George Cushing had revealed to his son all those years before, especially about Henry Cushing being a quantity surveyor. As Peter relates, "no mention of a quantity surveyor" in any of these documents. Peter also mentions some dates related to his grandfather, such as becoming a brewer's architect in 1899, a vocalist in 1907, and an actor (a "Tragedian") in 1912. In a roundabout way, Peter seems to accept these dates as accurate; however, Henry

Cushing died in April of 1899, thus making it impossible for him to have been involved in these avocations as noted by the dates. [12]

This situation takes us back to the question concerning how much Peter actually knew about his "Grand-dad" and his familial acting legacy while writing his autobiography. Since the above-mentioned dates are patently wrong, it is obvious that Peter's knowledge was moderate at best and that if he could have been told the whole truth, his astonishment would certainly have been great. Unfortunately, it is not known if Peter took the time to research his family acting history; however, he most definitely found the life of Sir Henry Irving worthy of his reading efforts. Some ten years ago at a Fanex horror film convention in Baltimore, Maryland, a certain professor told a group of horror film devotees that he possessed a very special copy of Bram Stoker's two-volume *Personal Reminiscences of Henry Irving*, published in 1906. On the flyleaf of the first volume, the signature of the original owner, along with that of his wife and a few sentimental lines, stands out in blue fountain pen ink. These signatures are by none other than Helen and Peter Cushing.

In a touching poem written for Helen in commemoration of their silver wedding anniversary in 1968, Peter waxes philosophically with the line "The Present stands on what the Past has taken." [13] Here is Peter's own admission that the past determines the future and that the decisions of those long dead often influence and guide the destinies of the living without premeditation. As Peter explains it, as a very young boy, he became enamored with Tom Mix, his favorite cowboy star, and "wanted to be like him when I grew up." Although not aware of it at the time, this was Peter's "lineal blood" stirring within him, "to follow in the footsteps of grandfather Cushing" [14] and those who came before him more than one hundred years prior to his birth in 1842. In essence, Peter's acting ancestors set a precedent for him to follow to become one of the most respected British actors of his generation, and if Henry Cushing could have known that his career as a stage performer would someday inspire his grandson to continue with the family acting legacy, he most assuredly would have been exceedingly proud.

§

I

Rogues, Vagabonds, and Scoundrels

In the year of our Lord 1737, when King George II ruled the mighty British Empire and his wife Caroline of Anspach, pleasant to the eye with a great love for reading and the witticisms of learned men, died at the age of fifty, the House of Parliament passed the Licensing Act which labeled every person "who shall for hire, gain, or reward . . . act, represent, or perform any interlude, tragedy, opera, play, or other entertainment for the stage" as a rogue and a vagabond and thus subject to any and all penalties and/or punishments deemed proper by the Law. [1] Also, the great Lord Chamberlain, the sole licensor of all plays performed within the city of London, Westminster, and elsewhere, and the official censor of all stage performances, "can prohibit the acting of any act, scene, or part, or any prologue or epilogue" at his discretion or as delegated by the Lord Chamberlain's Office. [2]

The overall goal of this act was to openly discourage actors and actresses from performing what the English Crown considered as bawdy entertainment, usually based on dramatic works considered as indecent and immoral by mostly uneducated, ignorant British commoners and powerful elders in the Anglican Church. As a result, producers, actors, actresses, and their managers were vilified by the public for endorsing and presenting plays that corrupted English society and led their audiences down the path of decadence. Of course, with the Lord Chamberlain in absolute control, all performers and producers were required to obtain a rather expensive license which meant that many "rogues, vagabonds, and scoundrels" were forced to seek out other types of employment or else face the possibility of imprisonment in the dank dungeons of the Tower of London.

Although the acting legacy of Peter Cushing began in the middle of the eighteenth century, circa 1740, his familial British ancestry dates back to a time when the profession of acting did not even exist, long before William Shakespeare and the Globe Theatre and even the throne of England itself. The first investigation into the ancestry of the Cushing family was conducted by Caleb Cushing (1800-1879), a Massachusetts State Representative and Attorney General of the United States during the administration of President Franklin Pierce (1853-1857). The crux of his research revealed that the Cushing family had originated in Norfolk, England, but after coming to the conclusion that genealogical work was much too complicated and time-consuming, Caleb Cushing turned his project over to H.G. Somerby, a well-known American genealogist based in London, sometime in the early 1840s.

Between 1851 and 1853, Somerby made numerous trips to the British Museum to examine ancient manuscripts, especially the Subsidy Rolls which detailed poll taxes paid by wealthy families of high social ranking. Somerby also consulted what are known as Herald Visitations or copies of wills with wax-sealed family coats of arms, parish records, and ancient deeds issued by estates and manors in Norfolk, some of which were fully owned by the Cushing family. As genealogist Warren G. Cushing points out, Somerby's efforts "were crowned with unexpected success," for he discovered that the Cushing family was one of the leading nobility families in Norfolk during the fifteenth and sixteenth centuries as "lords of numerous manors," thus making Peter Cushing a distant ancestral Lord, comparable to a Germanic Baron. [3]

In the mid 1870s, Caleb Cushing managed to retrieve the manuscript written by the late Mr. Somerby concerning his research on the Cushing family which he then turned over to Lemuel Cushing, a lawyer from Montreal, resulting in *The Genealogy of the Cushing Family*, published in 1877 [4] which traces the family back to Thomas Cushing of Hardingham, Norfolk, in the early fifteenth century. After Lemuel Cushing died in 1881, Frank Hamilton Cushing, curator of the Ethnological Department at the National Museum in Washington, DC, continued the investigation which yielded evidence that the Cushing family owned numerous manors in Norfolk during the eleventh and twelfth centuries, the same period of time when Robin of Loxley supposedly lived with his "merry men" in the forests of Sherwood as bandits and vagabonds fleeing from the law. Coincidentally, Peter Cushing played the role of the Sheriff of Nottingham, Robin's arch-nemesis, in the *Sword of Sherwood Forest* (1960), directed by Hammer's Terence Fisher.

One astonishing example comes from the original manuscript of Frank Hamilton Cushing:

> Generation #20—Peter Cushing, the son of Thomas (Cushyn) Cushing, was born in 1562 in Hardingham, Norfolk, and married Susan Hawes on June 4, 1584 in Hingham, Norfolk. Peter Cushing moved to Hingham circa 1600, the year in which the parish registers begin. He was probably one of the first Cushings to embrace the Protestant faith, for the wills of his father and eldest brother are in the Protestant form. [5]

As a side note, in 1638, Matthew Cushing (the son of Peter Cushing), his wife and five children, left Norfolk, England behind after some type of dispute with the Anglican church and headed for the Americas on the ship Diligent and after landing in Boston Harbor "immediately proceeded to their destination, Hingham, Massachusetts, so named after the Cushing family estate in Hingham, Norfolk." [6] In effect, Matthew Cushing who died in 1660 is the sole progenitor of all Cushings currently living in the United States.

Following Frank Hamilton Cushing's untimely death in 1900, his son James Stevenson Cushing completed his father's manuscript that primarily focused on the Cushing family in America. This 700 page-long work was published in 1905 under the title "The Genealogy of the Cushing Family," and in 1969, Allston T. Cushing of Pennsylvania published a sequel, covering the Cushings in America from 1905 to 1969. [7]

Historically then, the Cushing family, while enjoying the good life in their beautiful manor houses and most certainly taking advantage of what was known as serfdom during the High Middle Ages with bonded laborers in the fields, plowing the rich, fertile soil and harvesting crops and other foodstuffs for the manor house pantry, witnessed many episodes of great change and turmoil, such as the establishment of the Magna Carta in 1215; the turbulent reigns of Edward I "Longshanks" and Edward II; the onset of the devastating Black Death in 1348; the reigns of Richard III, Henry VIII, and the "Virgin Queen" Elizabeth I; and the rise of the greatest playwright and poet of all time, the "Bard of Avon" William Shakespeare who created the blueprint for English dramatic theatre. Not surprisingly, Cushing family ancestry even pre-dates the Magna Carta, for "In 1066, a large contingent of Cushings accompanied their relative William the Conqueror to the Battle of Hastings and defeated King Harald. After William crowned himself King of England, he allotted forty-two mansions and estates across Norfolk to his Cushing kinsmen." [8]

****

According to British biographer and literary critic Samuel Johnson, "When a man is tired of London, he is tired of life, for there is in London all that life can afford." [9] Since Dr. Johnson was also a steadfast admirer of English dramaturgy, London's stellar theatres during the eighteenth century were for him places of wonderment and enchantment. There was Sadler's Wells, Dorset Gardens, the Queen's Haymarket, Drury Lane, the Old Vic, and the Pantheon, along with dozens of smaller playhouses scattered about the city and only accessible through dark and dirty alleyways and side streets.

There was also Covent Garden that in 1732 "generally presented a miscellany of dramatic entertainment" in which music played either "an accessory part or none at all." [10] Under the management of John Rich, Covent Garden was architecturally small and could only be accessed by means of a narrow, street-level colonnade with a stage some twenty feet wide and forty-seven feet deep and lighted by four candle-bearing hoops. [11]

In 1738, after a long run of operas by George Frideric Handel, Covent Garden began to present straight dramatic plays with those of Shakespeare receiving top billing and a limited number of English Restoration plays, generally written between 1660 and 1700, that presented "contemporary life in much the same spirit as modern musical comedy" and often contained "grossness, fine witticisms, and other breaches of decorum." The authors of these plays were the first English playwrights to "depict mankind as leading an existence with no moral outcome," trapped in a world of unscrupulous persons who entertained no special prejudices regarding ethical behavior. [12]

Between 1748 and 1779, a direct descendant of Peter Cushing performed as an actor at not only Covent Garden but also smaller venues throughout London and the English provinces. This was John Cushing, born on January 20, 1719 at Hardingham, Norfolk, whose life outside of his career as a stage actor is completely unknown except for the place and time of his death (Liverpool, 1790), his marriage to actress/singer Mary Forbey, also from Norfolk, on February 14, 1752, and the names of his five children, all born in Norfolk between 1753 and 1772. His first stage appearance was on August 4, 1741 in the pantomime *Harlequin Sorcerer* as a witch, given at "Lee and Woodward's booth . . . during the Tottenham Court Fair." The advertisement for this performance lists him as Mr. Cushion, a dialectical variation of Cushing, but in April of 1742, another advertisement for the play *The Lying Valet* lists him as Mr. Cushing. Exactly why Mr. "Cushion" decided to change the spelling of his surname is not known. [13]

British theatre critic William Archer, writing in 1890, calls 1741 "a red letter year in the history of the English stage" when David Garrick made his first appearance at Goodman's Fields on October 19 in the role of Richard III and Charles Macklin portrayed the devious character of Shylock in *The Merchant of Venice*, also at Goodman's Fields, sometime in February. [14] Archer adds that during this particular year, the Licensing Act of 1737 "was scarcely yet in force" and had not yet resulted in the closure of the small theatres at Goodman's Field. [15] Incidentally, John Cushing also appeared in plays at Goodman's Fields at about the same time as Garrick and Macklin, but whether he was on friendly terms with these two giants of English dramaturgy remains open to conjecture.

Between May and September of 1743, John Cushing appeared in other London-based plays and pantomimes under the management of actor William Hallam, one of the first theatrical managers to organize "a completely equipped company of players and send them across the Atlantic" to the American colonies. [16]

In 1751, Hallam's company of players appeared at the Nassau Street Theatre in New York City and performed such popular plays as Shakespeare's *Hamlet*, *The Merchant of Venice*, and *Richard III*. Whether John Cushing was involved as an actor in this bold adventure to America is presently not known. It was also during this five-month stretch that Mary Forbey Cushing was first noted in the London papers, and throughout the 1740s, Mary and John Cushing appeared together in numerous plays under the management of Mr. Hallam.

It appears that John Cushing was also somewhat of an entrepreneur, for in May of 1743, he operated his own booth at the May Fair and produced *The Wandering Prince of Troy* in which Mary Cushing played the female lead. In September at the Southwark Fair, Cushing presented *The Blind Beggar of Bethnal Green* with his wife in the role of Arabella. This play was based on an old ballad of the same name written during the reign of Queen Elizabeth I and concerns the daughter of a baron who sells her family jewels to marry Henry de Montford, an early version of a Bohemian. This theatrical union of man and wife treading the boards is eerily reminiscent of Helen and Peter Cushing, due to being members of Sir Laurence Olivier's acting troupe during the Old Vic tour of Australia and New Zealand and appearing together in a production of Thornton Wilder's *The Skin of Our Teeth* in 1948. [17]

In 1745, Mary and John Cushing became permanent members of the Hallam Company. The list of plays in which they appeared is quite long and indicates that they remained highly popular for many years as top-notch stage performers. Some of the plays and/or musical pieces from this period include *The Beggar's Opera*, a ballad by John Gay in three acts; *A Bold Stroke for a Wife* by Susanna Centlivre, a satirical play with heavy anti-government and religious sentiments; *The London Merchant; Or, The History of George Barnwell* by George Lillo, a tragedy that recounts the corruption of a young man by a prostitute; and Shakespeare's immortal classics *The Tempest* and *Richard III* in which John Cushing played the lead roles. [18]

Between 1745 and 1746, Mary and John Cushing appeared in at least thirty-four different plays, mostly at Goodman's Fields, originally located in Whitechapel and opened to the public in 1727 by Thomas Odell, the deputy Licenser of Plays. [19] By this time, Cushing had established himself as a fine stage actor, but as Philip H. Highfill points out, since Cushing had gained much of his acting experience in the provinces, he was not considered as a major actor with successes in so-called patent houses sanctioned by the English Crown as legitimate theatrical venues. [20] Some of John Cushing's most prominent stage performances at Goodman's Fields during this time were *The Beggar's Opera* and Shakespeare's *Hamlet* as Horatio, *Henry IV* as Prince Hal, and *Richard III* as Richmond.

In November of 1747, the theatrical career of John Cushing reached new heights when he was offered a position at Covent Garden, perhaps the most popular patent house in the city of London, frequented on many occasions by English nobility and high-ranking members of British society. Less than a year later, Cushing became a full-time performer at Covent Garden; however, for reasons that remain unclear, he did not receive top billing as an actor and was often forced to take on roles beneath his talents and ambitions.

A possible scenario is that Cushing was up against some stiff competition, particularly with Lacy Ryan (1694-1760), another Covent Garden actor some twenty-five years older than Cushing, thus giving him seniority over his acting rival. This might explain why Cushing decided somewhat hastily to set up his own acting booth at Bartholomew Fair in April of 1749, where he produced a startling comic piece called *The Adventures of Sir*

Lubberly Lackbrains and His Man Blunderbuss. As Henry Morley describes it in *Memoirs of Bartholomew Fair*, this comedy focused on "the exquisite drolleries of Sir Lubberly and his Lady Constance" (played by Mary Cushing), replete with violins, oboes, bassoons, trumpets, and kettledrums. [21]

As noted in the *General Advertiser* newspaper, John Cushing returned to Covent Garden sometime around November of 1749 and appeared as Osric in *Hamlet*. Also, his wages were increased, for he was now being paid a hefty two pounds per week, while Mary had to be content with fifteen shillings a week. For the 1749-1750 season at Covent Garden, Cushing acted in no less than ten different plays, the most outstanding being *Richard III*, *Othello*, and *Romeo and Juliet*. In April of 1750, Cushing received the staggering sum of twenty pounds as his share for a benefit performance held in his honor. [22]

Between 1753 and 1774, John Cushing became a specialized actor, due to appearing in a number of plays by William Shakespeare at Covent Garden, such as *Romeo and Juliet*, *Much Ado About Nothing*, *The Merry Wives of Windsor*, *Macbeth*, *Coriolanus*, *Julius Caesar*, *Hamlet*, and *Henry IV*. His last stage appearance was on May 28, 1782 in *The Busie Body* by Susanna Centlivre who in her play epilogue hopes that "with good humour, pleasure (will) crown the Night" and that it will fulfill her simple theory that comedy was designed "not for reform but for laughter." [23]

In October of 1790, John Cushing died at the age of seventy-one; his actress wife Mary, however, "did not act at Covent Garden after 1752, presumably having died before him," possibly in 1751. [24] Altogether, John Cushing is a very shadowy figure whose career on the stage endured for more than forty years and allowed him to live a rather comfortable life in the borough of Lambeth. In fact, in 1746, he was able to either rent or own a house located at No. 3 Lambeth Street. Incidentally, Lambeth is just to the north of the borough of Wandsworth where Henry William Cushing resided in the 1890s. The most probable reason for this is that Lambeth, as well as Wandsworth, was home to many non-patent playhouses and a few patent houses, such as the Old Vic (which still exists today) during the eighteenth century.

Also, in the mid 1700s, these two boroughs south of the River Thames held annual fairs that lacked the legal authority and recognition of the English Crown, thus making them subject to the bylaws of the Licensing Act of 1737. Dorian Gerhold relates that in 1771, "players of interludes and other evil disposed persons" operated booths and boxes used for plays which encouraged "vice and immorality," such as heavy drinking and "committing outrages and disorders until two or three in the morning." [25]

During his tenure as an actor in London and the provinces, John Cushing associated with many actors of questionable character, the so-called "rogues and vagabonds" denounced by the Licensing Act of 1737. The most famous, outside of Garrick, Macklin, and Lacy Ryan, was John Rich (1681-1761), a "complete mimic whose genius was entirely confined to pantomime" or the ability to express thoughts and emotions without words.

One story relates that Rich, on his way to a tavern in a coach, leaped through an open tavern window just as the coach passed by it and landed inside the tavern unbeknownst to the coach driver. When the coach stopped a few miles down the road, the driver noticed that Rich had vanished from inside the coach. He then turned around, and as the coach passed by the tavern window again, Rich leaped through the window and into the coach. Rich then hollered at the driver who stopped and opened the coach door. The coachman, "petrified with fear, would not accept any money, then later exclaimed that the devil had been his passenger." [26]

Another was James Quin (1693-1766), considered as one of the best tragedians of the mid 1700s and a master of dramatic roles. In 1717, Quin was pursued into a tavern by a jealous rival who "threatened to pin Quin to the wainscot (i.e., the wall) with a sword if he did not immediately draw his own. Quin drew and kept on the defensive" until his rival became so excited, he "actually fell upon Quin's sword and died. Quin was tried and acquitted." [27] Then there was John Edwin (1750-1790), one of the most "extraordinary actors of dark comedy that the stage has ever possessed." Like many of his fellow "rogues and vagabonds," Edwin "with competence and enjoyment within his grasp, preferred living in discomfort and dying in beggary. He enfeebled his powers by excesses in brandy until he died degraded and worn with disease." [28]

Besides these and many other actors with a penchant for drinking and carousing, there were also playwrights, poets, producers, and semi-professional stage performers who had written plays in which Cushing appeared in various roles. For instance, there was Samuel Foote (1720-1777) who squandered two inherited fortunes on drinking, women, and gambling, and George Colman (1732-1794), manager of Covent Garden from 1767 to 1774, whose hedonistic lifestyle eventually drove him insane.

There is some indication that after the death of John Cushing, another "Mr. Cushing" made his first entrance as an actor at the provincial Theatre Royal in Windsor on June 15, 1813. The only evidence for this comes from a playbill held by the John Johnson Collection of Printed Ephemera which notes that a "Mr. Cushing" performed in *Mr. Betty*, a comedic song and dance routine; *The Village Lawyer*, a comedic farce; and *The Tragedy of Zara*, based on a play by Voltaire and composed by poet and dramatist Aaron Hill (1685-1750). Exactly who this particular "Mr. Cushing" was remains a complete mystery, for he is not even mentioned in Philip H. Highfill's seventeen-volume opus on British actors and actresses. However, it is conceivable that he may have been one of John Cushing's grandsons, either Mark Cushing (1787-1829) or John Cushing (1785-1865), making a bold but obviously short-lived attempt to follow in his grandfather's acting footsteps. [29]

It would be almost ninety years following the death of John Cushing in 1790 that another member of the Cushing family would decide to "tread the boards" as an actor and performer. But unlike his predecessor, Henry William Cushing would find himself working among some the greatest stage actors and actresses of the nineteenth century during a time when actors were still considered as "rogues, vagabonds, and scoundrels" despite their contributions to British culture and the advancement of the dramatic arts.

§

2

The Life and Times
of
Henry William Cushing

I n May of 1905, the ever opinionated playwright, novelist, and social commentator George Bernard Shaw was asked by an unidentified reporter how he felt about biographies on famous actors. "If you decide to write about the life of an actor," replied Shaw, "let us have the truth about the artist . . . the self-sacrificing truth. The artist sacrifices everything to his art, beginning with himself. But his art *is* himself, and when the art is acting, the self is both body and soul." [1] As a literary figure, Bernard Shaw is widely considered as a rival to William Shakespeare, due to plays like *Man and Superman* with its complex plot, multidimensional viewpoints, and comedic overtones "full of clever quips and witty characters" reminiscent of Oscar Wilde whom Shaw considered as a rival but on friendly terms. [2]

However, the plays of Bernard Shaw, much like those of Wilde, were regarded by critics and the general British public as "unfit for public discussion" and as shocking and heretical by the church, thus making Shaw the playwright a rogue and a vagabond despite his obviously brilliant mind and natural genius for literary creation. [3] But as fate would have it, Shaw was in the ascendancy of his literary powers in 1905 when British theatre was dominated by "real actors" and was seen as a legitimate way to earn a living, at least in the eyes of theatre audiences, theatrical owners and managers. 1905 also marked the passing of the original rogue and vagabond, Sir Henry Irving, whose death, much like that of Peter Cushing, signaled the end of an era in which actors relinquished everything to their art or as Shaw puts it, sacrificed "both body and soul."

In contrast to the days of Bernard Shaw, British theatre in the early years of the nineteenth century was in the doldrums, partially because of the continuing influence of the Licensing Act of 1737, still in force against actor, playwright, and manager alike and responsible for keeping British drama at a level comparable to vulgar mediocrity. As Laurence Irving relates, theatre managers circa 1830 were desperate for new material and were willing to travel to Paris and beyond to seek out new talent and plays written by playwrights completely unknown in Great Britain but popular in France. [4]

To make things worse, experienced stage performers were hard to come by and when found often demanded high salaries and a stake in the profits, something that Henry Irving would never have tolerated. Thus, by the middle of the nineteenth century, professional actors and actresses were the *de rigueur* of the day and the era of "rogues and vagabonds" was drawing to a close, not to mention the emergence of a new type of audience created by the wealth and prosperity of the Industrial Revolution in Great Britain.

In 1832, the year of the first Reform Act to be passed by the British Parliament, poet and playwright Edward Bulwer Lytton, an outstanding member of the House of Lords and perhaps the first British novelist to dabble in the genres of the occult and science-fiction, assisted in delivering a report to his colleagues in parliament that called for "the expansion of copyright in dramatic literature to give writers control of public performances of their plays" and an end to the monopoly held by the Crown over patent theatres via the strictures of the Licensing Act. Although fiercely opposed by the Anglican church and the House of Lords, the Dramatic Property Act became part of English law, making it possible for the creation of the Theatre Regulations Act which granted complete artistic freedom to all theatres and set into motion the restoration of English dramaturgy. [5]

At about the same time as the passage of the Theatre Regulations Act in 1843, a young boy, not much more than four years of age, was living with his aunt Sarah and uncle Penberthy, "a bearded, generous-hearted Celtic giant" with an oversized Celtic temper, [6] in the small parish of Halsetown in Cornwall, a rather dreary place with grey cobbled streets, whitewashed clapboard houses, a simple shop, an inn for food and drink, and a chapel, all set within a landscape of more dreariness with sullen moors stretching into the distance.

As the young boy recalls, playtime was a rambunctious event and often included rambling over desolate hills and climbing huge boulders along the seashore that bordered the Celtic Sea to the north and the Atlantic Ocean to the south. [7] This young boy also possessed a great love for actors and play-acting, pretending on many occasions to be a roving, mischievous prince straight from the pages of Shakespeare. But unfortunately, the great stages of London were far to the north, and it would be many years before the inquisitive and precocious John Brodribb would become a real actor under the stage name of Henry Irving.

While young master Brodribb was acting out his fantasies in the dreary moors of Cornwall, John Cushing and his wife Sarah were busy raising a brood of children, ranging in age from infancy to the early teens, in the far-flung rustic beauty of Norfolk in the area of Wymondham, where John Cushing was born in 1813 to William (Cushion) Cushing, Peter's great-great grandfather, and Charlotte Holiday. Their oldest son, Henry William Cushing, was born on January 12, 1842 in London, Saint Pancras, Soper Lane, first mentioned in historical records of 1257 as the property of the monastery of Christchurch, Canterbury, later destroyed in the Great London Fire of 1666. [8] Details related to Henry Cushing's early life in Norfolk are not available, yet it is clear that he spent most of his youth working in a farming community with his father, described as an agricultural labourer in the 1851 census, and his younger brother Thomas, born in December of 1852 in Whissonset, Norfolk. [9]

As might be expected, this type of rural environment was not at all favorable for acquiring even a simple education, for as Clarice Swisher observes, the majority of English farmers "saw little benefit in book learning for their sons;" however, because of the need for educated young men to work in the thriving business environment of London, "a number of country schools were set up, intended primarily for the education of the sons of farmers." [10]

Circa 1861, at the age of nineteen, Henry William Cushing made the fateful decision to leave the agricultural life of Norfolk behind and head for the city of London, where the Great International Exhibition was being held in South Kensington. This exodus is well-documented, for according to the 1861 census for the county of Norfolk, Henry Cushing was not living at his father's house which shows that he left Norfolk before the census was taken. [11] Exactly why Henry Cushing decided to leave his home in Norfolk is not clear, yet it is feasible that due to possessing a beautiful baritone singing voice, he took off on his own seeking employment in London. How his father reacted to his oldest son's choice of destinations in pursuit of a possible singing career can only be guessed at, but it was certainly not a positive reaction, due to the lingering attitude of farmers and simple country folk that entertainers were "rogues and vagabonds" who lived as non-conformist Bohemians.

On August 25, 1863, after settling in London in the area of Saint Pancras, Henry Cushing married his first wife Mary Pearson who apparently died some ten years later. This union produced two children: William Henry Cushing (the birth name of Wilton Herriot), the step-uncle of Peter Cushing and the source of his middle name, in 1866, and Albert Walker Cushing (a.k.a. uncle Bertie), born between October and December, 1869 in Saint Pancras.

As a stage actor, Wilton Herriot was highly respected and admired in the theatrical circles of London and appeared on a regular basis in the popular comedic farce *Charley's Aunt*. Some of the venues that Herriot frequented as an actor include the Royalty Theatre, where he performed as Jack Chesney in *Charley's Aunt* on March 21, 1892; the Globe Theatre (as its stage manager) in *Settled Out of Court* in June of 1897; and the St. James Theatre. On or about January 27, 1897, Herriot married Florence Augusta Wilkinson, an American actress and member of John Augustin Daly's acting company of New York City. In attendance at Herriot's wedding reception were Nellie King Cushing (Peter's mother and Herriot's step-mother) and Maude Ashton Cushing (Peter's aunt), along with Henry Cushing and his second wife Emily Day. [12]

As to Albert Walker Cushing, accurate documentation on his life is at best sketchy, but it is a fact that he left (or was advised to leave) England in 1901 as mentioned by Peter. This date has been verified through an immigration passenger list that notes his arrival in Sydney,

Australia, in early 1901, a common port of entry. Also, according to the 1910 Australian Electoral Rolls, Albert Cushing was a registered voter living in Cottesloe, Western Australia, a small resort town located between Fremantle to the south and Perth to the north. His place of residence is noted as "White House" on Warton Street, perhaps a boarding house, and his vocation as a fisherman. [13]

As Peter asks, "What heinous crime could (uncle Bertie) have perpetrated to deserve such a fate?" a reference to Albert Cushing's "banishment" by his immediate family. "They used to send convicts there!" adds Peter. [14] Ironically, Fremantle is home to what is locally known as "Fremantle Gaol," a large prison dating back to the 1850s, but since Albert Cushing arrived in Australia voluntarily, he was not a convict nor was he fleeing from the law. In effect, Albert Cushing vanished into the wilds of Western Australia and as Peter mentions was never heard from again. However, there is the high possibility that Albert Cushing married and had children, thus assuring that Peter Cushing's lineage continues to this very day somewhere in Australia or perhaps Great Britain.

After the death of Mary Pearson, Henry Cushing re-married, this time to Emily Day (1848-1912, Peter's paternal grandmother) on February 4, 1873 at St. Mary's Church, Battersea, in the borough of Wandsworth, just southwest of London across the River Thames. As a major industrial center dating back to the early 1600s, Wandsworth is historically known for its variety of mills, such as for processing corn, oil, malt, leather, paper, and copper, and in 1832, one particular mill for processing iron was operated by George Day and Sons, thus making it possible that Emily Day was born and raised in Wandsworth which would explain why her marriage to Henry Cushing occurred here rather than in Saint Pancras. [15] At various times during the nineteenth century, Wandsworth was home to a number of prominent personalities like the "Swedish Nightingale" Jenny Lind; Mary Ann Evans (a.k.a. George Eliot), author of *The Mill on the Floss*; poet and novelist Thomas Hardy; and an aspiring writer/journalist named H.G. Wells. [16]

Three children resulted from this second marriage for Henry Cushing—George Edward (b. July 1, 1881 in Saint Pancras), Maude Ethel (b. March 1884 in Saint Pancras), and Sydney Perceval in Wandsworth who died eleven weeks after his birth in 1885. Under her stage name, Maude Ashton is described by Peter as his "favorite aunt among a veritable tribe of such relatives" and as an outstanding actress at the Gaiety Theatre in London. [17] Peter also notes that he saw his aunt Maude in a one-act drama as a "lady of easy virtue" whose morals left much to be desired. [18]

Maude Ashton also specialized in comedic routines and was often in the company of Gertie Millar between 1905 and 1912. Born in Yorkshire in 1878, Millar started her acting career as a singer and dancer and was very popular in Yorkshire music halls. In London, she quickly became the "talk of the town" in two ways—first as a successful variety performer in the musical *Our Miss Gibbs* (with Maude Ashton), and second, as the source of a scandal in late October of 1905. According to *The Stage*, a weekly British theatrical newspaper established in 1880:

> The Deputy coroner for Central London conducted an inquiry at St. Pancras Coroner's Court into the death of Gunther Rau von Holzhausen, a German baron, aged about twenty-three who on Sunday morning last was found shot in the head in the boudoir of Miss Gertie Millar. Medical evidence showed that the deceased died from a bullet wound in the brain . . . self-inflicted. [19]

For her sake, Miss Millar was not at home when this event occurred, and exactly why this "German baron" committed suicide in her boudoir (a lady's private bedroom or dressing room) remains a total mystery.

Shortly after his marriage to Emily Day, Henry Cushing became a resident of Wandsworth, living at 55 Eglantine Road, an area of mixed poverty and upper middle-class comfort. Photographs of the period reveal that most of the houses in this area of Wandsworth were maisonettes, a French word for "small houses" or self-contained, two story apartments or flats located within a larger dwelling. Architecturally, the front door entrance of a maisonette usually faces the street and a set of stairs allows access to the apartment that might be above or below the entranceway. Living in this type of dwelling indicates that Henry Cushing's financial situation at the time of his marriage was moderate at best and that he may have been employed as a common laborer rather than as a quantity surveyor as mentioned by Peter. Curiously, in the early 1870s, the city of London was undergoing extensive alterations in the shape of new public buildings and private homes, some of which had stood for well over three hundred years, thus making the need for laborers especially high.

As John Summerson describes it, the years between 1860 and 1880 were boom times for architects, builders, quantity surveyors and estimators, and during this twenty-year period, "the architectural profession became more of a business and expanded rapidly on the bread-and-butter rather than the aesthetic side, and recruited largely from the lower to middle classes." However, highly-skilled and educated architects and quantity surveyors did not participate in these building activities on a large scale and there was no "distinct school of official architects" which kept salaries low for "freelance" quantity surveyors and the common worker. [20] It is interesting to note that a talent for higher mathematics, an essential prerequisite for a quantity surveyor, seems to run in the Cushing blood via George Cushing as a professional quantity surveyor. Whether Henry Cushing also had this talent is not apparent, but if he did, then it is reasonable to assume that he might have "freelanced" as a quantity surveyor without any formal education in this multifaceted occupation.

The earliest published report so far discovered on Henry Cushing as a professional stage performer comes from the pages of *The Era* for October 31, 1875 via *The Water Carrier*, based on Italian composer Luigi Cherubini's opera, at the Princess Theatre in London. On this particular night at the Princess, "the theatre was not merely full, it was densely crowded, not only for a mere ballad opera . . . but for a work which makes few concessions to popular taste." As to the composer, this opera represents "one of the lightest of his works, yet we are reminded at every moment of the great command of his art possessed by one whom Beethoven himself said is one of our greatest Italian composers." Although his role is not identified, Henry Cushing was "quite good and satisfactory" and gave just the kind of performance that was "required to show how high a standard could be reached with opera in English." [21]

The next reference is also from *The Era* for January 20, 1878 at Her Majesty's Theatre in a production of Irishman William Vincent Wallace's *Maritana*, a grand opera in three acts and based on the play *Don Cesar de Bazan* which served as the primary source for Massenet's comedic opera of the same name and which first appeared in Victor Hugo's novel *Ruy Blas*. In this opera, Henry Cushing performs as the Captain of the Guard, a minor role yet "amusingly represented" for the "tune-loving public" of Her Majesty's Theatre. [22]

The third item comes from the *London Times* via the classified advertisement section with news items on upcoming musical events and plays, along with theatrical commentary and reviews. This one is dated February of 1878 for Her Majesty's Theatre in London with Henry Cushing appearing in Charles Gounod's opera *Faust* in the role of Wagner, friend and confidant of Valentine and the brother of the heroine Marguerite.

Composed in 1858 in five acts and first performed in Paris a year later, *Faust* opens with the aged philosopher, tired and worn out from life's tragedies, in his private study, and upon hearing the voices of young people outside of his window, he calls on the devil to assist him. Soon, Mephistopheles appears and grants him great wealth and power, along with eternal youth in exchange for his immortal soul.

In Act II, Henry Cushing makes his first appearance and sings "a short solo in praise of drink" and then leads a crowd of revelers in the Song of the Rat. Moments later, Mephistopheles, the darkest of Satan's angels, "sways the crowd with the Calf of Gold aria, and then reads Wagner's palm, predicting an early death." When Wagner and the revelers come to realize his true identity, Mephistopheles "inscribes a circle around himself with a sword" which prompts Wagner and the revelers to "reverse their own swords so the hilts become the sign of the cross," forcing Mephistopheles to cower in terror. [23] An unidentified theatre critic for *The Era* observes that "Mr. Cushing was an efficient Wagner" and added considerably to the entire ensemble's performance. [24]

As shown by a rather long commentary by an unidentified critic for the *London Times*, Henry Cushing performed the role of Wagner (which calls for a baritone in Gounod's list of characters) several times during "the brief winter season of opera in English" in 1878:

In a generally effective performance of *Faust*, Mr. Talbo (Faust) exhibited a marked improvement with a voice worth seriously cultivating. The other characters are filled by Signor Franceschi (Mephistopheles), Mr. George Fox (Valentine), and Mr. H.W. Cushing (Wagner). The general performance may fairly be commended. [25]

Although it is very likely that Henry Cushing appeared in some type of musical entertainment prior to 1875, supportive evidence is wholly lacking. However, it is known that at some point, he became a client of James Henry Mapleson, a well-known British theatrical agent and manager who supplied singers for the opera houses of London from about 1861 to 1887. According to his obituary, published in the *London Times* on December 27, 1901, Mapleson was perhaps the most successful manager of Her Majesty's Theatre which helps explain Henry Cushing's repetitious appearances at this lavish venue, established by architect and playwright John Vanbrugh in 1705 as the Queen's Theatre which presented operas by Handel and Mozart and which currently serves as the home of Andrew Lloyd Webber's ultra-successful *The Phantom of the Opera*. [26]

Mapleson also managed other highly popular venues within the city of London, such as Covent Garden, the Theatre Royal in Drury Lane, and even the Lyceum Theatre. As an entrepreneur, Mapleson held much responsibility for the construction of the National Opera House on the River Thames Embankment in 1877, and in his memoirs, Mapleson notes that this magnificent building "was devoted to the presentation of Italian opera and to the production of the works of English composers with English performers, both vocal and instrumental." [27] In 1887, due to high financial costs related to upkeep and repairs, Mapleson sold the building to the Metropolitan Police which then erected New Scotland Yard on the site.

The next published report on Henry Cushing's involvement in an opera is dated September 25, 1883 at the Crystal Palace in French composer Daniel Auber's *Fra Diavolo*, another comedic opera in three acts and based upon the exploits of Neapolitan (i.e., southern Italy) bandit Michele Pezza, a.k.a. "Brother Devil." In this piece, Henry Cushing portrayed Giacomo (fifth billing) and is described as "rendering efficient service" to the talents of the ensemble. Another unidentified theatre critic for *The Era* notes that all of the performers in this opera were more than sufficiently applauded "with the utmost enthusiasm, and some of them were even encored." [28]

This appearance was followed by another opera at the Crystal Palace on October 17, 1883, a version of Giuseppe Verdi's three-act extravaganza *La Traviata*. Once again, Henry Cushing's role is not mentioned, merely as "Mr. Cushing," but in the cast of characters for this opera, set in Paris during the reign of King Louis XVI, there appears only one role for a baritone—Giorgio Germont, the father of Alfredo and the lover of Violetta, a courtesan or prostitute. At the time of this performance, Henry Cushing was living in Saint Pancras rather than Wandsworth at 25 Willes Road, another medium income maisonette or walk-up flat, where George Edward Cushing was born in 1881.

There is also a reference from *The Era* that describes a very odd production called *Paw Clawdian*, a sort of operatic Roman burlesque with British actor John Lawrence Toole as "Paw" Clawdian Andlivates, a "horrid profligate" from Byzantium who does not allow any man to say "that he is an upright Roman." In this strange production at Toole's Theatre (formerly the Folly Theatre in London) on February 16, 1884, Henry Cushing performed the role of Sesiphon (seventh billing) whose relationship to "Paw" Clawdian is not stated in the article. One of Cushing's fellow performers in this "not too pretentious, not too long . . . good, honest, wholesome fun" production was George Shelton, an apparent master of the "Irish Tetrarch" style of singing who was both "clever and diverting" during the show. As it turns out, Shelton was present at Henry Cushing's funeral in April of 1899 which demonstrates some type of abiding friendship between them as professional stage singers. [29]

The final notice of Henry Cushing's performance in an opera is dated June 3, 1886 in another comedic piece known as *Simpson and Delilah* by Henry Sutherland at the Avenue Theatre Playhouse in Northumberland, London. This time around, Cushing received tenth billing without any indication of his role. Thus, it appears that Henry Cushing's career as an opera singer was winding down after almost a decade of fine baritone work in some of the world's best operas and at a number of London's most prestigious venues. Stylistically, Henry Cushing certainly had a flair for comedy and comedic singing which seems to have been inherited by his children as stage performers during the very early years of the twentieth century. Family-wise, Maude Ethel Cushing arrived in March of 1884, joining three year-old George and step-brothers Albert Walker and Wilton Herriot.

In his memoirs, John Henry Mapleson writes at length about his tours to the United States, beginning in October of 1878 and concluding in late 1886, noting that the first American tour was composed of 140 individuals with sixty of these comprising "a magnificent chorus of selected voices." [30] During this eight year-long stretch of touring the States in such cities as New York, Boston, Philadelphia, Chicago, and Cincinnati, some of the greatest Italian operas of all time were performed by Mapleson's company of singers, including *Carmen*, *Don Giovanni*, *The Marriage of Figaro*, and *Rigoletto*, along with various German and French operas and some variations on Shakespeare's *Hamlet* and *Othello*.

Also in his memoirs, Mapleson provides short biographies on his major and minor players, but unfortunately, Cushing the opera baritone is not even mentioned. But as luck would have it, Henry Cushing's obituary for April 22, 1899 in *The Era*, a weekly London newspaper similar to *The Stage* but with more general news and announcements, relates that he "visited the States under Colonel Mapleson eighteen years since," meaning that Cushing performed in America during the second tour that began in October of 1881 in New York City, perhaps at the prestigious Metropolitan Opera House. [31]

As an opera singer, Henry Cushing was under the management of "Colonel" Mapleson for more than eight years and it seems that he may have parted ways with his longtime employer for financial reasons. In the reminiscences of Luigi Arditi, an Italian conductor, composer, and musical director of Her Majesty's Theatre from 1857 to 1878, Mapleson "paid his debts when he had money, but when the safe was empty, he knew how to rid himself of tiresome and embarrassing debts with remarkable graciousness" and never allowed those who were owed a salary "to depart uneasy at heart." [32] If Henry Cushing was owed a considerable amount of salary for past performances, then his decision to leave Mapleson's operatic company is understandable, especially with small children at home and having to pay rent for a three-room walk-up in Saint Pancras.

Less than a year after leaving Mapleson's employment, Henry Cushing became a standing member of Sir Henry Irving's Lyceum acting company. The date of April 2, 1887 has been verified through a notice in *The Era* that places Cushing at a Lyceum Benevolent Fund dinner at the Freemason's Tavern, presided over by Henry Irving. At this dinner to raise funds for struggling actors, the song "Wine, Wine" was "admirably rendered by Stewart, Tabb, and Cushing." [33]

Thus, the year 1887 was not only pivotal for Henry Cushing but also for English literature which entered a new phase of development known as the Victorian transitional period, highlighted by the reading public's growing fascination with the supernatural and the fictional genres of mystery and horror. In 1887, Arthur Conan Doyle introduced the great detective Sherlock Holmes and his partner in crime detection Dr. Watson in *A Study in Scarlet* which unbelievably was rejected by two major London publishers (Arrowsmith and Warne & Company). The third publisher, Ward, Lock, and Company, also rejected it at first but then relented when Doyle accepted twenty-five pounds for the copyright. As John Dickson Carr relates, the wife of the head editor at Ward, Locke, and Company was highly enthusiastic about the novel. "This man is a born novelist!" she remarked. "It will be a great success." [34]

There was also *She* by H. Rider Haggard, first published in serial form in 1886 and then as a novel in 1887. Bibliophile of the fantastic Donald A. Wollheim once observed that Haggard's *She* is "a classic of the imagination, a milestone and foundation stone for a whole sector of fantastic novels upon which other have built and still build novels of wonder." As to the character of Ayesha, the "She" of the novel, Wollheim reminds us that "She" "is no hideous and frightening creature; she is a marvel of matchless beauty, a thing of untold powers, immortal and not to be touched" by the hands of man. As "She" herself admits as the white goddess of the lost city of Kor, "My empire is of the imagination." [35]

Also in 1886, Scotsman Robert Louis Stevenson introduced one of the most influential novellas of the late nineteenth century—*The Strange Case of Dr. Jekyll and Mr. Hyde*, "a conception essentially out of time and place" and undoubtedly "one of Stevenson's greatest achievements" as an author and speculator of the unknown. Allegedly conceived during a dream, *Jekyll and Hyde* could be described as an allegorical attempt to relate "the tale of a man who was two men" and as the ultimate embodiment of "the duality of man's nature," [36] split into two separate beings, one good, the other evil, through a powdered concoction instead of the familiar chemical potion in film versions of Stevenson's novella.

According to legend, Henry Irving was so struck by the power of Stevenson's *Jekyll and Hyde* that he seriously considered playing the dual role on the stage of the Lyceum Theatre. If this had actually occurred, then the theatrical and film history of Stevenson's horror masterpiece would have turned out very differently. In fact, Irving's personal attraction to this tale of the doppleganger with its macabre characterizations was so profound that he invited American actor Richard Mansfield, "a melodramatic actor of some power . . . who took himself and his work intensely serious," to appear at the Lyceum in the dual role of Jekyll and Hyde during the summer months of 1888. [36] For some unexplained reason, *Jekyll and Hyde* at the Lyceum failed to generate a large and profitable audience, perhaps because of Stevenson's indifference to having his material adapted for the stage. [37]

Shortly after Mansfield's unsuccessful run in *Jekyll and Hyde* at the Lyceum, a run-down section of London called Whitechapel began to dominate the headlines of all the major papers in the city, due to a series of extremely bizarre and terrifying events in Whitechapel's fog-enshrouded back alleys and pitch-black streets. On September 14, 1888, the *London Times* reported that a prostitute named Annie Chapman had been found murdered in the backyard of a house on Hanbury Street with her throat cut from ear to ear and her body horribly mutilated. A response in the prestigious medical journal *The Lancet* concerning the murder of Miss Chapman denied the accusations that a homicidal maniac was responsible for the crime. "The theory that the succession of murders," relates the report, "which have lately been committed in Whitechapel are the work of a lunatic appear to us (as) not well-established." [38] Five weeks later, the *London Times* attached a name to this supposed lunatic via a letter posted to the London police—"Jack the Ripper"—now synonymous with terror and depravity and to this very day unidentified despite more than a hundred and twenty years of investigation by "Ripperologists," conspiracy theorists, and modern-day forensic experts.

On March 23, 1889, Henry Cushing attended another event at the Freemason's Tavern, this time a special supper to raise funds for the Lyceum Theatre. Presided over by Henry Irving with acting manager and personal secretary Bram Stoker at his side, Cushing and his fellow Lyceum comrades toasted Irving and then devoted "the remainder of the evening to music and recitation which were continued until four o'clock on Wednesday morning." Part of this after-supper entertainment was provided by Stoker via "Irish recitations" and Cushing who sang "The Hunter's Farewell." [39]

Clearly, Henry Cushing's employment under Irving completely altered his career as a professional stage performer and placed him into direct contact with some of the leading stage personalities of the day, such as Ellen Terry, Johnston Forbes-Robertson, William

Terriss, and John Martin Harvey. One important consequence of Cushing's membership in Irving's company is that he became close friends with several secondary Lyceum performers and with actors outside of the sphere of Irving and his magnificent show palace on the Strand who were willing help him along the way in relation to building upon his professional resume.

Perhaps his closest friend and most ardent supporter was William Sydney Penley, born at St. Peters, Isle of Thanet, Kent on November 19, 1852 and educated at his father's school on Charles Street, Westminster, in London, where he studied music and singing with the Chapel Royal Choir and served as a chorister at Westminster Abbey. In 1875, while residing at 34 Cologne Road, Battersea, in Wandsworth with his actress wife Mary and daughter Lizzie, Penley became a member of an opera company owned and operated by Richard D'Oyly Carte, manager of the Royalty Theatre in Soho and responsible for bringing together Gilbert and Sullivan for a one-act, operatic drama called *Trial by Jury* with Penley playing the role of the jury foreman. Penley's employment with D'Oyly Carte's opera company spanned more than sixteen years with an occasional leave of absence to work with other opera companies and theatre owners in London. During this time, Penley became a well-respected and admired stage performer and was widely recognized for his ability to play dramatic as well as comedic operatic roles.

On October 29, 1883, Penley appeared at the Royal Comedy Theatre in a three-act operatic comedy called *Falka* in the role of Brother Pelican. [40] In August of 1884, Penley appeared at the Globe Theatre, Newcastle Street on the Strand, in the ever-popular *The Private Secretary* as Reverend Robert Spalding, a role once played by Herbert Beerbohm Tree, a famous contemporary of Henry Irving. [41] On September 3, 1886, Penley was at the Globe Theatre again in *The Pickpocket*, a farcical comedy with Penley receiving second billing. [42] A year later in November of 1887, Penley returned to the Globe in another comedy *The Arabian Nights* as Joseph Gillibrand. As reported in *The Stage*,

> It is almost impossible to describe the fun extracted by Mr. Penley from a very small part. Dressed in very tight trousers and a very horsey short coat, Mr. Penley has only to pose to create abundant laughter. During the last act, Mr. Penley sat down at the piano and accompanied Miss Vennie in "I Was In It" to which he added a chorus of his own invention. [43]

By 1889, Penley's popularity as a comedic actor and singer brought him to the steps of the Lyceum Theatre, where he appeared in *Aesop's Fables* as Horace, a role that elicited roars of laughter from the audience. [44] However, Penley's "big break" occurred in February of 1892 with *Charley's Aunt*, yet another comedic farce produced by Penley at the Theatre Royal in Drury Lane. Originally written for Penley by his friend Brandon Thomas, *Charley's Aunt* became a huge success, running for almost 1,500 performances at the Theatre Royal and later at the Globe in 1893. According to his obituary in the *London Times* for November 12, 1912, Penley's role as Lord Fancourt Babberley in *Charley's Aunt* was one of the most "mirth-provoking performances of the 19th century," due to "an extraordinarily droll little man with a delicacy of mind and touch that saved him . . . from exaggeration and vulgarity." [45] In essence, *Charley's Aunt* made Penley a well-to-do man, for it was rumored that he pocketed more than two hundred thousand pounds over the course of the play's run in London.

Playing hundreds of times alongside Penley in *Charley's Aunt* was Wilton Herriot, Peter Cushing's step-uncle and the oldest son of Henry Cushing. Peter himself considered his step-uncle as quite mysterious, much like uncle Bertie, and relates that as a "tragic actor," Herriot was married twice, a subject "regarded as unsuitable for my youthful ears." [46] The friendship between Penley and Herriot appears to have been quite strong, due to the fact that Herriot served as stage manager at the Globe Theatre for many years and in 1895 during the height of Penley's success in *Charley's Aunt* wrote the play *A Little Ray of Sunshine* in which Penley appeared numerous times. [47]

Since William Penley and Henry Cushing performed in various operas and musical productions concurrently between the early 1870s and 1880s, it was inevitable that their paths would cross at some point, especially because Richard D'Oyly Carte, Penley's manager, and James Henry Mapleson, Cushing's manager, moved within the same operatic circles and had business relations with the same owners and managers of venues like the Theatre Royal, the Alhambra, and Her Majesty's Theatre with Mapleson as its operational manager. Of course, it is also highly probable that Wilton Herriot introduced his father Henry Cushing to William Penley at some point during his tenure with Penley at the Globe Theatre.

By the early 1880s, the friendship between Penley and Henry Cushing had turned into something very special, due to discovering a unique shared connection in the form of the Lodge of Aspah, number 1319, a London-based Masonic organization created in 1870 "for the convenience of members of the dramatic and musical professions." Within the records of the Library and Museum of Freemasonry in London, Henry Cushing the "vocalist" was initiated into the Lodge of Asaph on January 7, 1884, passed on February 4 by the highest-ranking members of the lodge, and raised on March 3 to a permanent member. [48]

As described by Dennis V. Chornenky, president of the Masonic Restoration Foundation, the initiation proceedings experienced by Henry Cushing would have been a "slow and sensitive process that requires great effort on behalf of the candidate and the existing members of the lodge." Chornenky adds that in order for initiation and Masonic growth to be meaningful and enriching,

> Great care and attention must be afforded to each individual candidate. He must understand that the organization is highly selective (which) allows him to feel self-worth and leads him to respect the high standards of the Order. He must also

be effectively educated about the history, symbolism, and philosophy of the Craft if he is to become a Freemason worthy of the title. [49]

In all respects, the Lodge of Asaph (from the Hebrew for "God has gathered") was a special Masonic entity because all of its members were linked to the performing arts, whether as singers, actors, musicians, producers, set designers, or playwrights. During what was (and still is) known as an installation meeting, held on an annual basis, the "brethren" of the lodge would discuss new business matters, install new members, and elect long-standing brothers to important posts, such as "Worshipful Master," "Pro-Grand Master," and "Deputy Grand Master." As part of this ancient ritual, members participated in "loyal and Masonic toasts" to "the Queen (Victoria) and the Craft" and the "Worshipful Master" would present gifts or specially-made Masonic badges and medals to former lodge Masters for their contributions to the Craft.

After the close of the installation meeting, various brothers would entertain their fellow "brethren" with poetic recitations which in Henry Cushing's time were written by famous Freemasons like the eternal poet laureate of Scotland Robert Burns, Robert Morris (the Poet Laureate of Freemasonry), novelist Rudyard Kipling, and on occasion by members of the lodge. On special occasions, a member might recite the Masonic Sermon with its philosophical tenets to "adore the Grand Architect of the Universe;" "Do good for the love of goodness itself alone;" "Fly from the wicked, but hate no one;" "Read and profit, see and imitate, reflect and labor;" and "Respect the stranger on his journey and assist him, for his person is sacred to thee." [50] There were also songs and instrumental performances and more often than not, a large banquet rounded out the festivities.

During the days of Henry Cushing's membership in the Lodge of Asaph, this ritual was followed by yet another gathering, usually at the Freemason's Tavern with more drinking, singing, and general carousing among lodge members and selected visitors. As to drinking, all of the lodge "brethren" were to "enjoy themselves with decent mirth" and were not allowed to force "any Brother to drink beyond his inclination." One ancient toast sums it all up—"Here's a health to our Society and to every faithful Brother that keeps his oath of secrecy." [51]

Regarding Penley's initiation into the Lodge of Asaph, George Rowell notes that it occurred on March 5, 1883; one month later, Penley was passed by the lodge and on May 7 was raised to a true "brethren." His dedication to the lodge seems to have been so deep that he was made "Worshipful Master" in 1892. [52] On November 7, 1885, Penley attended a meeting and a banquet at the Lodge of Asaph with Henry Cushing [53] and in 1886 was invested as an officer and served as its unofficial organist. [54] Penley and Cushing also attended the annual Lodge of Asaph meeting in November of 1889. [55] Therefore, it is quite obvious that Penley introduced Henry Cushing into the rites of the Lodge of Asaph, due to being initiated in March of 1883, ten months before his good friend and fellow thespian.

William Penley also belonged to many other Masonic lodges in London, such as the Yorick Lodge, number 2771, as its "Worshipful Master" in 1901; the Pen and Bush Lodge, number 2909, as its "Worshipful Master" in 1902; the Green Room Lodge, number 2957, as treasurer, and the United Grand Lodge of England in 1903; and the Lyric Lodge, number 3016, in 1904 as the inaugural "Worshipful Master." [56] Penley was also a member of the Savage Club, founded in 1857 by a group of authors, journalists, and artists in order to provide "an informal but private venue for members of London's Bohemia" or those who enjoyed convivial entertainment with much food and drink. Much like the Lodge of Asaph, the Savage Club was only open for "gentlemen connected professionally with literature, art, and drama," and by 1887, the official and consecrated Savage Club Lodge had initiated more than a hundred "Bohemians" via the rites and rituals of Freemasonry. [57]

One of the most outstanding members of the Savage Club Lodge was Henry Irving, a regular and steadfast supporter of many Masonic charities, Masonic schools, and the Royal Masonic Benevolent Institution. Although Irving warmly supported the principles and ideals of Freemasonry, "the pattern of his Masonic career makes it clear that he never took a very active part" in Masonic activities, perhaps because of his commitments at the Lyceum Theatre as manager, producer, and actor. However, Irving viewed the Savage Club Lodge as an excellent organization that deserved to be recognized for its activities related to helping the poor and the under-privileged. [58]

In the spring of 1890, one of the greatest classics of Gothic horror fiction appeared in the pages of *Lippincott's Monthly Magazine* of Philadelphia—*The Picture of Dorian Gray* by Irishman Oscar Wilde, a name forever linked to the deepest mournfulness of the human soul, the "gleaner of *fleurs de mal* (flowers of evil) who brings to mind that creation of Hawthorne's weird fancy, the fungus brilliant but fatal which can only grow from a dead man's heart." [59] When *The Picture of Dorian Gray* was published in England by Ward, Lock, and Company (the same entity as *A Study in Scarlet*) in 1891, it was greeted with a storm of protest by critics who unanimously condemned it as the work of a depraved mind without scruples or any sort of affection for the "Grand Architect of the Universe." [60] Wilde's novella was also savagely criticized for its depiction of a handsome young man who trades his soul for eternal youth, a theme much in line with Marlowe's *The Tragical History of Doctor Faustus* and Charles Gounod's opera *Faust* of which Henry Cushing was of course quite familiar.

While the critics raged against Wilde's masterpiece of the macabre, Henry Cushing made one of his first appearances at the Lyceum Theatre in the historical romance *Louis XI* by Irish-born playwright and occasional actor Dion Boucicault. As Madeleine Bingham observes, Henry Irving's interpretation of King Louis XI of France (1423 to 1483), one of history's true Machiavellian princes and a possible witness to the burning at the stake of the doomed Joan of Arc, was full of "sardonic humor, irritable passion, and alternating cruelty," helped along by grotesque makeup that evinced the pale and cadaverous face of a man known for his web of deceit as the "Spider King." [61] Running from May 19 to May 23, 1890,

Louis XI brought Henry Cushing into the wondrous world of the Lyceum as Monseigneur de Lude with William Terriss as Nemours and a number of Lyceum regulars like F.H. Macklin, Henry Howe, John Martin Harvey, and John Archer, all of whom (excepting Terriss) were members of the Lodge of Asaph.

Cushing's next role was as the Commissary of Police in *The Lyons Mail* by Charles Reade who allegedly "borrowed" the plots of many important European novels by renowned authors like Victor Hugo and Emile Zola for his plays. Running for twelve performances between February 7 and April 25, 1891, *The Lyons Mail* plots out a true case of mistaken identity related to the disappearance of a large sum of money from a mail carrier intended as payment for Napoleon Bonaparte's troops fighting in the Italian Campaign of 1796.

Resplendent with cold-blooded murder, armed robberies, shootings, and devious plot twists, this play featured Irving in the dual roles of Joseph Lesurques, mistakenly identified as the thief of the payroll, and Dubosc, the actual payroll bandit. British theatre critic Clement Scott interprets Dubosc as "a relentless demon and a common murderer" [62] who views those in his sphere of influence as obstructions to his plans and goals. Ironically, Scott's interpretation of Dubosc is very reminiscent of Peter Cushing as the Baron in *The Curse of Frankenstein* and *Frankenstein Must be Destroyed*.

Perhaps as a way of emulating his employer, Henry Cushing found great pleasure in helping the less fortunate members of his profession. This is not to say that Cushing was financially stable, for as Donald Mullin informs us, with the exception of performers like Ellen Terry, Johnston Forbes-Robertson, William Terriss, and actor-managers such as Henry Irving, "ragged starvation was commonplace" for actors and actresses alike. [63] Nonetheless, on June 24, 1891, Cushing attended the first annual dinner of the Actor's Benevolent Fund at the Metropole Hotel in London with Irving as chairman. At this particular event, Henry Cushing donated ten shillings (half of a pound) to the fund which may seem like a small amount but at the time was enough to pay for a comfortable room at one of London's finest hotels. Also in attendance was Ellen Terry, playwright A.W. Pinero, Charles Dickens, Jr., and Bram Stoker. [64]

For almost all of 1892, totaling two hundred and four performances, Henry Cushing played the role of a secretary in *King Henry VIII* at the Lyceum Theatre. Based on William Shakespeare's play and first produced at the famous Globe Theatre in 1613, *King Henry VIII* was undoubtedly Irving's greatest exhibition of theatrical pageantry with historically accurate costumes and stunning sets and backdrops designed and painted by Hawes Craven, Joseph Harker, and William Telbin.

In this production, Cushing played the secretary to Irving's Cardinal Wolsey and shared a few scenes with William Terriss as King Henry VIII. He also shared some lines with Johnston Forbes-Robertson as the Duke of Buckingham and Ellen Terry, "the living embodiment of the Raphaelite woman," [65] as Queen Katherine. As if two hundred and four performances in this play was not enough work, Cushing also appeared in *Richelieu*, based on the political exploits of French clergyman Cardinal Armand Jean du Plessis de Richelieu (1585 to 1642), as the Captain of the Guard with Irving as the Cardinal and William Terriss as De Mauprat. [66]

In April, Cushing's admirable penchant for providing as best as he could financial relief to his fellow actors was satisfied at the annual supper of the Lyceum Provident Fund, similar to the Actor's Benevolent Fund but geared toward assisting "comrades" of the Lyceum experiencing financial difficulties. As usual, Henry Irving was chairman of the supper and after proposing a toast to the "Health of the Queen," he thanked all of the members of the fund for their contributions and noted how delightful it was to see them all together at the Freemason's Tavern. Following supper, the remainder of the evening was devoted to music and recitation with Cushing and seven other members singing a variation on Mendelssohn's "Love and Wine." The main attraction at the conclusion of the evening was "informal entertainment" with Cushing performing some type of musical arrangement supported by ten other members, one being Bram Stoker. [67]

By 1893, the theatrical career of Henry Cushing had escalated considerably, due to appearing in revivals of *Louis XI* in April and May; *The Lyons Mail* from April to June; and *King Henry VIII* during the middle of July in which Cushing's role as a secretary was replaced by the larger role of Sir Nicholas Vaux. In effect, Cushing was a very busy actor, performing in four major plays between February and the end of July. The most significant was Alfred Lord Tennyson's *Becket*, based on the tragic relationship of King Henry II Plantagenet and Thomas Becket, the archbishop of Canterbury from 1162 until his assassination at the hands of the king's hired men in 1170. In this play, Cushing is billed as the Bishop of Hereford with William Terriss as King Louis of France, John Martin Harvey as Lord Leicester, and Ellen Terry in the role of Rosamund.

The overwhelming stress during this period in Henry Cushing's theatrical career was lessened considerably by Queen Victoria who summoned Henry Irving and the entire cast of *Becket* to the opulent Waterloo Gallery in Windsor Castle for a private performance of the play. Along with the queen in attendance was the Empress Frederick of Germany who later recorded in her diary that Victoria "treated the players with every consideration" and allowed them the rare treat of a private audience. Bram Stoker, the ever-faithful servant to Sir Henry and every member of the Lyceum Company, is said to have been emotionally overtaken by the queen's caring nature and her obvious respect for Irving and the cast of *Becket*. [68] Thus, as a successful stage actor with very humble beginnings in the agrarian countryside of Norfolk, Henry Cushing could boast of having met Queen Victoria whose love for the theatre and even "rogues and vagabonds" like Cushing, Irving, Harvey, and Terriss, made all of the hardships and disappointments more easy to bear and perhaps more laughable.

Due in part to the great popularity of *Becket* with English audiences, Henry Irving began to prepare for his fourth American tour in mid 1893, first by revising the most popular plays from the Lyceum's repertoire and then putting together a stellar cast that Laurence Irving refers to as an "expeditionary force" composed of more than eighty performers in addition to a chorus master, a harpist, musical director, and an organist. [69] This was Henry Cushing's first opportunity as a member of the Lyceum Company to tour the United States which at the time was under an economic depression brought about by corporate greed and the unregulated power of industrial monopolies owned and operated by the so-called "Robber Barons" like John D. Rockefeller, Andrew Carnegie, J.P. Morgan, and Cornelius Vanderbilt.

For this ambitious tour, Irving and his players focused on three plays that Irving felt would attract the largest audiences and put much-needed funds into the shrinking coffers of the Lyceum—*Becket*, *Henry VIII*, and *The Bells* with Irving as Mathias, a murderer driven to madness by the ringing of sleigh bells. Some of the cities scheduled for this tour included San Francisco, Seattle, Minneapolis, Chicago, and New York City, where *Becket*, just as Irving had figured, grossed over $6,000 on its opening night at the Abbey Theater. [70]

On July 9, prior to his departure to America, Henry Cushing attended a special dinner in honor of Henry Irving at the Grafton Galleries on Bond Street, a colossal four-story edifice with galleries displaying artwork by some of the most prestigious artists of the period. In total, one hundred and twenty guests attended this dinner, a sort of farewell party for Irving and his Lyceum Company before sailing off to America. Some of the Lyceum players in attendance included Gordon Craig, the son of Ellen Terry; John Martin Harvey who joined Irving's acting troupe in 1882 and remained for fourteen years; Henry Howe; Harry Brodribb Irving, Sir Henry's eldest son; Laurence Irving; A.W. Pinero; Johnston Forbes-Robertson; R.P. Tabb; William Terriss; and John Lawrence Toole. "God Speed to Henry Irving!" was the main toast which was received with great enthusiasm. [71]

Upon returning to England in early 1894, Henry Irving and his Lyceum Company of actors and actresses found the British government in turmoil, due to the resignation of Prime Minister William Gladstone and the appointment of Archibald Philip Primrose, Lord Rosebery as his replacement. There was also trouble brewing about Ireland and its longtime struggle for Home Rule or independence from Great Britain which Gladstone wholeheartedly endorsed. But in keeping with his desire to bring high-quality entertainment to the audiences of the Lyceum, and perhaps as a way of diverting attention from the realities of political life in England, Irving re-introduced the most terrifying production of his career, W.G. Wills' *Faust*, a derivative spin-off of Marlowe's 1592 masterpiece *The Tragical History of Doctor Faustus*.

Originally presented at the Lyceum on December 19, 1885, this updated version of the Faustian legend wherein a learned scholar sells his soul to the devil for a life bountiful with beautiful women, wine, and debauchery, opened on April 14, 1894 with some of the most elaborate special effects ever devised for the Victorian stage, such as "magical appearances and disappearances through trap doors, sulphurous infernos and brimstone" reminiscent of Hades, huge arrays of electrical lights and calcium arcs that simulated lightning, and steam engines under the stage that generated clouds and walls of fog. [72] Dominating the stage was Irving as Mephistopheles, dressed in a vivid, blood-red costume and a long, flowing scarlet cape. According to biographer Austin Brereton, Irving's rendition of Mephistopheles, enhanced by the garish scenery of Craven and Telbin and surrounded by swirling vapors excited by the calcium arcs, was akin to the Devil himself whom "men and women might expect to meet if ever the Prince of Darkness crossed their paths." [73]

Alongside Henry Cushing as a citizen, there was William Terriss as Faust, John Martin Harvey as Frosch, R.P. Tabb as a soldier, and Ellen Terry as Margaret, a young girl with a soul damned by Faust and the Devil and doomed to eternal hellfire. [74] With some seventy-six performances of *Faust* behind him by July of 1894, Henry Cushing had clearly come to understood the rigorous demands of acting. "The pressures upon players were enormous," observes Donald Mullin, and "emotional or physical breakdown at an early age was routine." [75] Not surprisingly, one of Irving's maxims for all actors under his employment was that they must never forget that "excellence can only be attained by arduous labor, unswerving purpose, and unfailing discipline," [76] and as Gordon Craig notes in his 1930 biography, Irving the "taskmaster" rehearsed his actors unceasingly and worked for hours upon the stage with his actors, sometimes from early morning to long past midnight, especially if a play like *Faust* was to be presented on the following afternoon. [77]

As to financial compensation for all of his dedicated work, Henry Cushing received what would now be considered as a nominal salary. For example, a Lyceum salary list indicates that Cushing was paid three pounds, ten shillings (three and a half pounds) for his work during 1896. In today's U.S. dollars, this equals to approximately $413. In contrast, Ellen Terry received two hundred pounds which equals in today's dollars to about $23,000. Salaries for other Lyceum performers during this period ranged from a low of two pounds (approximately $240) to a high of twenty-two pounds (approximately $2,500). If we take into consideration the rate of inflation since 1896, Henry Cushing's annual salary would be in the range of $40,000, [78] thus placing him firmly within the British middle classes.

During the waning months of 1894 and well into 1895, Henry Cushing reprised his roles in *Becket* (this time as John of Oxford), *Faust*, *Louis XI*, and *The Lyons Mail*. In July of 1895, Cushing also appeared as an attendant in a magnificent production of Shakespeare's seminal masterpiece *Macbeth* with Irving in the lead role, John Martin Harvey as Lennox, and Ellen Terry as Lady Macbeth. For some unexplained reason, contemporary accounts and critical notices on this production are almost non-existent, but as biographer Charles Hiatt describes it, "enormous pains were spent over the staging of this tragedy" in the form of true-to-life scenery that replicated to the smallest detail Scottish medieval castles and interior halls, producing "a sense of absolute illusion." [79]

On June 4, 1895, Henry Cushing and more than eighty of his Lyceum colleagues assembled for their annual social meeting at the Freemason's Tavern to support the Lyceum Theatre Provident Fund with as usual Henry Irving as chairman and organizer. Among the guests were Henry Howe, H.B. Irving, Bram Stoker, R.P. Tabb, and John Martin Harvey. After a sumptuous dinner and much conversation, Irving proposed a toast to Queen Victoria and then to the Prince and Princess of Wales (Albert Edward, the son of Queen Victoria, and Alexandra of Denmark), whom Irving noted were "warm and constant patrons" and shared a "liberal sympathy with the dramatic arts." After other toasts to Irving and the health of the fund, Cushing participated in a group rendition of the song "Absence" by John Liptrott Hatton. Along with piano accompaniment, this musical piece calls for soprano, alto, tenor, and bass vocalists with Cushing supplying the lower register. Also joining Henry Cushing at this dinner was his son Wilton Herriot. [80]

Although toasting "Old Vic" was not an uncommon event during her reign which lasted from June, 1837 until January, 1901, Henry Irving had much to celebrate in July of 1895 when Queen Victoria granted him knighthood, thus making him Sir Henry. In a lengthy reminiscence by Arthur W. Pinero, a member of the Lyceum Acting Company from 1876 to 1881 and a respected playwright, the knighting of Henry Irving benefited and advanced the social standing of every actor and actress in Great Britain and proved to the general British public that actors are hard-working and dedicated professionals, thus effectively dimming the antiquated image of stage performers as "rogues, vagabonds, and scoundrels." [81]

On August 31, Henry Cushing embarked on his second visit to the United States as part of Sir Henry Irving's fifth American tour. An unidentified occasional reporter for *The Era* wrote that Irving's company of Lyceum players included John Martin Harvey and his wife Angelita Helena Margarita de Silva Ferro, and an entire roster of lesser-known Lyceum actors and actresses, totaling more than seventy, all under the guidance and direction of Bram Stoker. Out of these seventy plus Lyceum regulars, almost half were wives, such as Mrs. Allen, Mrs. Holland, Mrs. Lacy, and Mrs. Cushing. [82]

This "Mrs. Cushing" was Emily Day Cushing, Henry's second wife and the mother of George and Maude Cushing. In a customs report for August 11, 1895, issued by the Collector of Customs for the city of New York regarding passengers aboard the S.S. Southwark, Emily Cushing identifies herself as an actress, forty-five years of age.

As frustrating as it is, no evidence has been found to support the idea that Emily Cushing was a member of Sir Henry's Lyceum Acting Company; however, a clipping from the *London Times*, dated October 25, 1884, mentions a "Miss Cushing" as a member of the Royal English Opera Company; another item from *The Stage* lists Emily Cushing as a contributor to the Actor's Benevolent Fund in January of 1891, only six months before Henry Cushing attended the first annual dinner of the fund at the Metropole Hotel in London. [83] Since Emily Day Cushing was obviously involved in the theatre, this opens up the tantalizing possibility that Henry's first wife Mary Pearson may also have been an actress or a member of an operatic company.

Sometime in early November while still "on the road" with his fellow Lyceum performers in America, Henry Cushing attended a makeshift Lodge of Asaph meeting at the Winthrop Hotel in Boston, Massachusetts. In a cablegram written by F.H. Macklin and read aloud at the 25th anniversary meeting of the Lodge of Asaph at Freemason's Hall in London on November 9, the "Worshipful Master" highlighted that Cushing and six other members were drinking to the health of the "Worshipful Master" Charles Cruikshanks and wished him a long and happy life. "We drink to our brave brothers and fair sisters" read the cablegram, "and though absent from you in body, we are with you in spirit." In response, Cruikshanks pledged a toast to his "absent friends" in Boston and then read another cablegram from Macklin:

> Perhaps in a few years time one may be able . . . to propose a health through the telephone. It is very interesting to participate in conviviality in a country that charges five dollars a bottle for champagne. We also appreciate the Americans good qualities, especially when they see us drinking to them in bumpers (large drinking vessels) at midday. [84]

Sir Henry Irving's fifth American tour stretched into May of 1896 with a final two-week engagement at the Abbey's Theater in New York City. By early August, the entire Lyceum company had returned to England, and almost as soon as his feet touched the shores of his beloved nation, Henry Cushing went back to work at the Lyceum Theatre. His first appearance of 1896 was in Shakespeare's *Richard III* as Cardinal Bouchier that ran from December 19 until April 7, 1897 for a total of thirty-five performances. In addition to Sir Henry as the hunchbacked Richard III, there was Gordon Craig as King Edward IV, John Martin Harvey as Robert Brackenbury, F.H. Macklin as the Duke of Buckingham, and R.P. Tabb as the Lord Mayor of London. In spite of Sir Henry's sinister portrayal of King Richard III, a few critics derided him by referring to his performance as cheap and detached; however, J.F. Nisbet, a highly-regarded critic for the *London Times*, exclaimed that Irving's Richard III was "the most satanic character I have ever seen on the stage." [85]

On November 1, 1896, Henry Cushing, as was his habit, attended another meeting of the Lodge of Asaph at Freemason's Hall, but this time around was accompanied by "Wm. Herriot" or William Henry Cushing, a.k.a. Wilton Herriot, proving beyond any doubt that Herriot was now a Freemason like his father, due to being an entertainer, singer, and actor. Following the usual adjournment of this meeting and after rejoining at the Freemason's Tavern, "brother" Samuel Johnson (no relation to the famous British author and essayist) gave a lengthy speech to his fellow "brethren" that highlights how Cushing and other members of the Lodge of Asaph felt about "the Queen and the Craft":

The virtue, grace, and dignity of her Majesty . . . has been frequently alluded to from the Master's chair of the lodge, not only on account of her interest in the Craft, but particularly for the great and abiding interest she has always taken in the material prosperity of the musical and dramatic professions. Not long ago, she granted knighthood to the acknowledged head of the dramatic arts in the person of Sir Henry Irving, an honour richly deserved by him. Among the subjects that might be referred to in proposing a toast, many might be selected, but one cannot be avoided . . . that her Majesty has now accomplished the longest reign of any British sovereign. [86]

At this juncture in Mr. Johnson's speech, Henry Cushing must have been exceedingly pleased with his "boss" Sir Henry Irving, due to knowing that he had participated in some of Irving's greatest theatrical achievements over the course of a decade at the Lyceum Theatre. Interestingly, after Irving was knighted in 1895, the English Crown bestowed this honor on other members of the Lyceum Acting Company, such as Johnston Forbes-Robertson in 1913 whose son John Forbes-Robertson appeared in Hammer's *Legend of the Seven Golden Vampires* with Peter Cushing, and John Martin Harvey in 1921. As to her "Majesty," Cushing's emotional response to hearing such praise from Mr. Johnson must have moved him deeply, considering that Queen Victoria was the only reigning head of state he had ever known in his life.

Mr. Johnson then concluded his remarks by noting that Queen Victoria had done much for not only the dramatic arts but also for the Empire and Freemasonry in England:

Her reign has been distinguished by great progress in the prosperity of the country and in the great strides made in art and science, and in the extension and expansion of the British dominions. It is particularly gratifying to Freemasons that wherever the British flag has been planted, Masonry has been established and has flourished. [87]

Lastly, Mr. Johnson felt it was necessary to say something about the profession of acting:

When I began to study Freemasonry, I went into it heartily, and through my own experience, derived at a very early age in the theatrical profession, I realized that no man could succeed unless he thoroughly went into his business. An actor must thoroughly understand the author's intentions before he can perform the part allotted to him. This I know is clear to all of my brethren of the Lodge of Asaph who truly understand the circumstances of an actor's life. [88]

In May of 1897, one month after Henry Cushing's final appearance as Cardinal Bouchier in *Richard III*, Bram Stoker was in the middle of preparations for a special performance at the Lyceum Theatre. On the 18th, this performance or "reading" of Stoker's material which was "partially hand-written and partly pasted into place in sections cut from two proof copies" was witnessed by employees of the Lyceum Theatre who surely must have thought Stoker had lost his mind, due to the stage being completely bare of props and scenery. Through some sort of machinations on his part, Stoker persuaded fifteen supporting Lyceum actors and actresses to read the various "roles" written (or better yet, scribbled) on pages with large gaps in the text and in some instances partially obscured by blotches of ink. [89]

This reading on May 18 was a pre-copyright production of *Dracula* which Stoker had been working on for the better part of ten years. The "role" of Count Dracula was read by T. Arthur Jones, a secondary bit actor on the Lyceum payroll and a member of John Martin Harvey's theatrical company, thus making Mr. Jones the first actor to "play" the character of Count Dracula. For reasons that have never been fully explained, Sir Henry Irving refused to participate in this first reading of *Dracula*; however, he apparently found it interesting enough to witness the reading on the morning of May 18.

As Barbara Belford relates, Stoker came to Irving in his dressing room and asked, "Well, how did you like it?" Irving's response was "Dreadful!" Thus, "Despite the countless hours Stoker spent trying to persuade Irving to be Count Dracula," Irving flatly refused "to consider a role that would have set the standard for any future interpretation" of Stoker's bloodsucking Master of the Undead. [90] It is fascinating to think of what might have been if Irving had agreed to read the part of the Count and perform as Dracula, dressed in ebony with a long, flowing cape and lurking about the stage in the manner of the person who was to become the quintessential Count Dracula some thirty years later—Bela Lugosi.

In many ways, Bram Stoker's *Dracula* symbolized the culmination of Gothic fiction in Great Britain during the final decade of the nineteenth century and remains today as the unsurpassed representative of horror fiction with a vampire as the main antagonist. However, another work of Gothic horror fiction published at the same time as *Dracula* (perhaps within a few months of each other) somehow slipped through the proverbial cracks and is now virtually ignored by readers and literary scholars alike.

In *The Blood of the Vampire* by English novelist Florence Marryat who died in 1899, the same year as Henry Cushing, the central character is a beautiful female vampire (shades of Le Fanu's *Carmilla*) named Harriet Brandt, the daughter of a high-ranking British colonial administrator and a Caribbean priestess with an inclination for practicing voodoo. However, this vampiric female refrains from drinking blood; instead, she draws life from the living by touching her victims. Also, Miss Brandt, much like Carmilla, exudes "simple, innocent, virginal goodness" that draws victims to her, particularly men, children, "and a scheming Baroness" who corrupts Harriet's innocence for her own evil intentions. [91]

Beside her career as a novelist, Florence Marryat was also an opera singer. Between 1882 and 1884, Marryat appeared in numerous operas while under the management of Richard D'Oyly Carte's Opera No. 2 "Patience" Company, the same entity as William Penley who appeared as Reverend Robert Spalding in *The Private Secretary* at the Globe Theatre in August of 1884. Whether Marryat and Penley ever crossed paths during their operatic careers is open to speculation.

For Sir Henry and his troupe of actors and actresses, and for the general British public, December of 1897 marked two important landmarks. First, it was the nineteenth anniversary of the Lyceum Theatre under the management and direction of Sir Henry Irving; and second, the reign of Queen Victoria was in its fiftieth year and after months of preparation, the nation was ready to celebrate the Queen's Diamond Jubilee. But unfortunately, on the night of December 16, William Terriss, a long-standing member of Irving's acting company and highly esteemed for his roles as Cassio in *Othello* and Mercurio in *Romeo and Juliet*, was murdered by Richard Prince, a small-time bit actor, at the Adelphi Theatre in Maiden Lane, the Strand, where Terriss often performed and served as its manager.

As the story goes, Prince was fired by Terriss for his heavy drinking, and due to being unemployed, Prince sought out financial assistance from the Actor's Benevolent Fund which was granted after Terriss recommended it to the fund's council. On the afternoon of December 16, Prince showed up at the offices of the fund to collect his money but was told that the council would not meet until the next day. At this point, Prince became convinced that Terriss had stiffed him by having his name removed from the list of beneficiaries for the fund. As darkness fell, Prince waited until Terriss arrived at his private entrance to the Adelphi Theatre for his evening performance. As Terriss was about to enter the theatre, Prince emerged from the shadows and stabbed him three times with a dagger, killing him almost instantly.

At his trial, Prince was found guilty of the murder of William Terriss; however, the judge declared him insane and committed him to Broadmoor Criminal Lunatic Asylum for the remainder of his natural life. Sir Henry, one of Terriss' closest friends, and almost every actor in London became extremely upset over Prince's relatively light sentence. Shortly before the trial, Sir Henry allegedly told the press that because Terriss was an actor, Prince would not end up at the end of the hangman's noose which turned out to be dead-on accurate. [92]

In concert with the murder of William Terriss, Henry Cushing seems to have made his last appearance on the Lyceum stage in *Madame Sans Gene*, a play by Victorien Sardou which has been aptly described as an historical romance of the French Revolution of 1792 with Irving as Napoleon Bonaparte, Ellen Terry as Catherine, Cushing as De Fontanes, and many familiar Lyceum actors and actresses in other roles, such as F.H. Macklin, John Martin Harvey, and Norman Forbes, the son of Johnston Forbes-Robertson. [93]

Overall, this production was quite successful; in fact, as Laurence Irving recalls, the proceeds from this play "very nearly restored the balance of the Lyceum accounts" which made Sir Henry very happy. There were also plans to present *Peter the Great* at the Lyceum with Ethel Barrymore, the sister of the great John Barrymore, in a major part. [94] 1897 was also a busy year for Wilton Herriot. On February 25, he appeared as Dick Burton in *Confederates*, a drama in one act by Henry Woodville, at the Globe Theatre; on May 1, he reprised his role in *Confederates*, also at the Globe; and on June 3, Herriot appeared as Francois in *Settled Out of Court*, a play in four acts by playwright and actress Estelle Burney, at the Globe. [95]

The absence of documentation in reference to Henry Cushing's appearances in additional plays at the Lyceum Theatre after December of 1897 does not necessarily mean that he retired from the stage at the relatively young age of fifty-five. Instead, it seems that his health was deteriorating rather quickly, leaving him unable to continue working in the craft he so dearly loved. Exactly when Cushing's health began to decline is not clear, but he apparently was in good enough shape to attend Wilton Herriot's wedding and reception in January of 1897.

In some ways, Henry Cushing's deteriorating health was a blessing in disguise, for right around the end of 1897, British theatre was evolving into a different kind of entertainment known as "New Drama" which emphasized a natural style of acting as contrasted with flamboyance and exaggeration in the style of Sir Henry Irving who firmly believed that acting was not suppose to imitate reality. As J.O. Bailey explains it, acting was an artform, a type of "sublime poetry expressed in gesture, tone, and declamatory power," but by the late 1890s had shifted to a natural approach via the imitation of reality, also known as realism. [96]

For Henry Cushing, adapting to this new style of acting may not have been possible, due to being so accustomed to (if not guided by) Sir Henry's acting style and the demands of the Shakespearean mode of presentation. But just across the English Channel in the city of Paris at 44 Rue de Rennes, a new form of entertainment was about to eclipse live theatre, thanks to the Lumiere Brothers and their machine known as a cinematographe. This of course was a motion picture projector, a crude instrument but capable of taking an audience into a world never seen before via moving pictures that were seemingly alive.

By 1898, the stage career of Henry Cushing was over and it appears that he was now spending most of his time at his home in Wandsworth at 55 Eglantine Road (the same maisonette in 1873, possibly owned by his wife Emily's family), where he had relocated from Saint Pancras sometime around 1895. Also, for Sir Henry and his Lyceum Acting Company, the end of everything almost came to fruition, for in February, tragedy struck when all of the expensive scenery and stage properties amassed by Irving over a twenty year period went up in flames in a storehouse. In total, two hundred and sixty scenes were destroyed, along with beautifully rendered backdrops by Hawes Craven and William Telbin.

For Sir Henry, this was a staggering loss, so much so that the great Lyceum company never fully recovered. As Laurence Irving sums it up, on the morning of the fire, Sir Henry arose from his bed to "find himself stripped of the resources upon which his hopes" had been set for a new era in the theatre, compounded by a steady decline in his physical energy. [97] The same could be said of Henry Cushing, most probably bedridden with all of his physical resources dwindling. Perhaps a few lines from Thomas Hood's poem *The Dream of Eugene Aram* is appropriate:

> All night I lay in agony,
> In anguish dark and deep;

My fevered eyes I dare not close,
But stare aghast at sleep;
For sin has rendered unto her,
The keys of Hell to keep. [98]

In early 1899, Sir Henry Irving, facing mounting debt and experiencing much pain as a result of pneumonia and pleurisy, made the momentous decision to sell off his interests in the Lyceum Theatre, thus relieving him of all financial responsibility and turning over the Lyceum to a syndicate. Bram Stoker, Irving's longtime acting manager and personal secretary, was utterly dismayed by this decision to the point where their twenty-five year-long friendship became strained if not ruined. But Irving's recuperative powers made it possible for him to remain active on the stage for another six years until October 13, 1905 when he died from the effects of a stroke and physical exhaustion at the age of sixty-seven.

On April 12, 1899, Henry William Cushing died at his home in Wandsworth at the age of fifty-seven. The exact cause of his death is not known, but according to a brief notice in *The Era* for April 15, Henry Cushing died as the result of a "long and painful illness" [99] which might help explain why his acting career faltered during the mid 1890s, due to being too ill to carry on with his work. If we suspect that the exact cause of his death was some form of cancer, it might not be too far from the truth since the habit of smoking was widespread in late nineteenth century Britain. Thus, lung cancer seems to be the best choice. Here is Henry Cushing's funeral notice from *The Era*, April 22, 1899 in its entirety:

The funeral of Mr. Henry William Cushing, whose death on the 12th we announced last week, took place on Saturday afternoon at Wandsworth Cemetery. The chief mourners were his eldest son, Mr. Wilton Herriot; his third son, Mr. George Edward Cushing; Mr. G.F. Barnes, executor; Mr. Robert J.S. and Mr. T. Bradford; Mr. Stewart Bradford; and Mr. Walter Reynolds. Also in attendance were the deceased's colleagues at Carlton Chambers; his comrades at the Lyceum; Mr. and the Miss Gardner; Mr. and Mrs. George Shelton; Mr. and Mrs. William Sydney Penley; Mr. Stewart and Mr. Percy Bradford; the Rev. Father Cooney; Mr. William Bradford; Mr. and Mrs. Walter Reynolds; Mr. George Barnes; Mrs. Wilkinson; Miss Verrier; Miss Randall; Mr. and Mrs. R.P. Tabb; Miss Sidney Rutter; and Miss Elsie Brettingham. Crosses from Mr. and Mrs. Bartlett and family; Mr. J.B. Marsh; and one from his younger sons and daughters. A lyre, with strings of Parma violets, was sent as a last tribute from his devoted son and daughter-in-law (Mr. and Mrs. Wilton Herriot). The deceased actor was for some fifteen years associated with Italian and English opera, and in 1887, joined Sir Henry Irving's Lyceum company of which he continued to be a member until his death. He visited the States under Colonel Mapleson, eighteen years since, and was there three times with Sir Henry Irving. [100]

As one might suspect, most of the individuals mentioned in Henry Cushing's funeral notice were actors with links to each other and the Lyceum Theatre, such as George Shelton, a close friend of Penley and Herriot and a secondary performer in dramatic and comedic plays like *The Tree of Knowledge* (1897 to 1898), *Mr. Sympkyn* (1897) at the Globe Theatre along with Penley and Herriot in *Confederates*, and a version of J.M. Barrie's *Peter Pan* (1917 to 1918) with actress Fay Compton, best-known for playing Mrs. Sanderson in *The Haunting* (1963); and R.P. Tabb, a member of the Lyceum Acting Company who appeared on stage with Cushing in *Richard III*, *Louis XI*, and *Henry VIII* and was a standing member of the Lodge of Asaph. It should be mentioned that Cushing's funeral notice states that he toured America three times with Sir Henry when in fact it was only twice, being the fourth and fifth tours.

This notice also makes reference to Cushing's "colleagues at Carlton Chambers," an area in London dominated by Regent Street that runs through Soho with Wigmore Street to the north and Piccadilly to the south. In the 1890s, many types of businesses were located in Carlton Chambers, such as artist studios, solicitors, real estate agents, merchants, and insurance companies; there were also private homes of wealthy upper-class families and architectural firms that required the services of quantity surveyors. In his autobiography, Peter Cushing wonders how his grandfather "managed to be an actor as well as a quantity surveyor," due to both professions "requiring one hundred percent of one's time." [101] Whether these "colleagues" at Carlton Chambers were architects is not known, but an important slice of information confirms that Henry Cushing was not an official quantity surveyor. According to Joyce Condon, information officer of the Royal Institute of Chartered Surveyors, an organization that includes as its members quantity surveyors, Henry William Cushing is not present in any of its extensive records.

A discerning eye will observe that Emily Day Cushing and Maude Ashton Cushing are not mentioned in the funeral notice. The reason for this absence may be related to an epidemic of influenza that struck England and Wales in 1899, killing more than 12,000 persons. Also, Henry Cushing's "comrades" from the Lyceum Theatre are only represented by R.P. Tabb. Where, one might ask, are the rest of them? Surely, at least a handful would have taken the time to attend the funeral of one of their own from the Lyceum. However, this can be attributed to the fact that Cushing's funeral took place on Saturday afternoon, April 15, a very busy day at the Lyceum Theatre with the entire cast of *Robespierre*, numbering some seventy individuals, rehearsing for the opening night performance. Therefore, it would have been difficult if not impossible for even a dozen Lyceum players to leave the theatre and attend Cushing's funeral. [102]

Compared to actors like Johnston Forbes-Robertson, John Martin Harvey, Gordon Craig, William Terriss, and other top-billed male performers under the management of Sir Henry Irving, Henry William Cushing was a secondary figure, ranked in the dramatis personae of numerous playbills at sixth billing or lower down on the list. But Cushing was not alone, for as Donald Mullin observes, "a very large number of players whose names are recorded for a season or two" eventually slipped back into "the obscurity from which they arose." [103]

But Henry Cushing managed to remain active on the stage as an opera singer and actor for almost twenty-five years and did an excellent job at adapting to the rigors of stage life. In the end, it is unfortunate that Henry Cushing did not live long enough to enjoy the birth of his grandson Peter Wilton Cushing in 1913 and to his amazement witness Peter's growing interest in the theatre as a young boy. As Christopher Gullo sees it, Henry Cushing's "unexceptional impact on the acting profession would someday yield a more substantial benefit" [104] in the shape of Peter Cushing, born to be an actor and "tread the boards" like John Cushing in the 1700s and his "Grand-Dad" at the Lyceum Theatre.

§

Bram Stoker, ca. 1890

Michael Gough, early 1960s

Helen and Peter at home, early 1950s

SIR HENRY IRVING, LATE 1880S

PETER IN *I, MONSTER* (1970)

SIGNED PETER CUSHING CARD,
LATE 1950S

PETER IN HIS ROSE GARDEN,
WHITSTABLE, CA. 1969

Sir Henry Irving, mid 1890s

WILLIAM TERRISS, LATE 1880S

PETER DURING HIS DAYS WITH HARRY HANSON'S COURT PLAYERS, 1938

JOHN MARTIN HARVEY, MID 1880S

The Jewel
of the Lodge
of Asaph ribbon

The Cushing family Coat of Arms
(courtesy David Cushing)

Virtute et Numine

WILLIAM SIDNEY PENLEY
AS *CHARLEY'S AUNT*, 1892

SIGNED GERTIE MILLAR POSTCARD, MID 1880S

THE BLACK MILL IN WHITSTABLE, CA. 1900

COVER OF SOUVENIR BOOKLET FOR *BECKET*, 1893

A young Bram Stoker, 1884

PETER CUSHING AT HOME, EARLY 1970S

3

The Moon in June
is
Full of Beauty

A
s shown through the lives of John Cushing and Henry William Cushing, the life of an actor is by no means a casual walk in the park, meaning that along the way one encounters obstacles that appear to have been placed there on purpose. But when it comes to Peter Cushing, these obstacles simply had to be moved a few feet to either side in order to proceed down the path toward success as an actor. Of course, Peter possessed one important advantage that most of his contemporaries lacked—an inherited impulse to entertain, to "tread the boards" as the old saying goes as a professional performer. As he admits, Peter recognized this "latent desire" at a very young age, almost as if his ancestors were calling out to him from beyond the grave to take up the acting mantle and continue the family tradition.

If we compare the acting career of Henry William Cushing with that of his famous grandson, several important differences are immediately noticeable. First of all, Henry Cushing's career on the stage was relatively brief, spanning less than twenty years from about 1878 to 1897, while that of Peter endured for fifty years, beginning in 1936 at the Connaught Theatre in J.B. Priestley's *Cornelius* and ending with the sci-fi film *Biggles: Adventures in Time* in 1986. Second, despite being in the company of the great Sir Henry Irving and appearing in some of the most spectacular productions ever held at the Lyceum Theatre, the acting career of Henry William Cushing was not a stellar success, for he never achieved top billing and his salary for a month's worth of work never exceeded three or four pounds. In contrast, the acting career of Peter Cushing was a resounding triumph, for it eventually allowed him to earn a very good living as one of the top British box-office stars of his generation and to become an undisputed icon of horror cinema.

Lastly, Henry William Cushing possessed a strong inclination for acting and was certainly quite talented, considering his transition from an opera singer to an actor which by itself is quite a feat. However, Peter Cushing was more than just talented, for he was gifted beyond measure and excelled in many areas related to the arts. In 1924, Joseph Harker, one of the best scenic painters of the nineteenth century and responsible for the beautiful backdrops for *The Merchant of Venice*, *Ravenswood*, and *King Henry VIII* (and allegedly the inspiration for Jonathan Harker), wrote that his employer Sir Henry possessed "peculiarities of personality that marked (him)" from his contemporaries in relation to talent. Harker adds that Irving "seems to have been endowed with some mysterious magnetism of character" that defies analysis. [1] Likewise, Edward Gordon Craig, the son of Ellen Terry and frequently seen performing besides Sir Henry, notes that all great actors act by design and consciously avoids everything which does not reveal true art. Irving "was not merely fond of his art," says Craïg, "his art of acting was his religion." [2] The same could be said of Peter Cushing who considered the art (or craft) of acting as a gateway to spiritual enlightenment.

＊＊＊＊＊＊＊＊＊＊＊＊

On the morning of May 26, 1913, a hundred and twelve actors, actresses, and stage managers gathered together in the lobby of the beautifully restored Pabst Grand Circle Hotel in New York City with the intention of creating a union for American stage performers. The need for such a union was great, due to circumstances that actors were forced to endure on a daily basis, such as rehearsing for long hours without pay; having to provide for their own transportation if they ended up stranded in the middle of nowhere; paying for their own meals and lodging; and putting up with physical and emotional abuse from producers who still viewed actors as degenerates and social outcasts. One of these actors was Broadway star William Courtleigh who suggested a name for this new union—the Actors' Equity, still in existence today with almost 50,000 members. Oddly enough, actress Ethel Barrymore, recruited by Sir Henry Irving to perform in *Peter the Great* in December of 1897 just before William Terriss was murdered by Richard Prince, became the union's symbolic "Spirit of Equity." [3]

As Courtleigh and the new members of the Actor's Equity union celebrated at the Pabst Grand Circle Hotel, Rupert D'Oyly Carte, the second son of Richard D'Oyly Carte, was tending to the rigorous demands of the famous London-based D'Oyly Carte Opera Company, and from all contemporary accounts, it seems that Rupert was quite the businessman, due to operating not only the opera company but also the luxurious Savoy Hotel and several other high-class establishments in the city of London.

However, Rupert's business talents paled in comparison to those of his step-mother Helen Lenoir D'Oyly Carte, a quite exceptional woman for her time who "immersed herself in all of the business affairs" of her husband following his death in 1901 and gradually surpassed him "in her grasp of detail, organizational ability, diplomacy, and acumen." [4] Helen Lenoir's command of the D'Oyly Carte Opera Company and hotel business was unfortunately short-lived, for on May 5, 1913, she died at the age of sixty, leaving her step-son Rupert in complete control of the D'Oyly Carte Opera Company and all of the D'Oyly holdings, estimated at the time to be worth in excess of two million pounds.

Monday, May 26, was also a very busy (and certainly delightful) day in the middle-class household of George and Nellie Cushing, due to the arrival of their second son, Peter Wilton Cushing. For David Henry Cushing, born on June 27, 1910 in Eastbourne and Peter's older brother, this particular event certainly brought him much happiness, for he now had a constant companion who later on around the age of three would begin to exhibit a keen interest in art, literature, and play acting. A very enticing artifact, long concealed from prying eyes by a simple piece of cardboard, reveals a rare moment in the early life of David Cushing. On the reverse side of the original backing for a small watercolor done by Peter in 1930, a faint inscription, probably in the handwriting of Nellie Cushing, reads "David Henry Cushing," then some height and weight measurements, "Aged nine months," and then "To his Aunt and Uncle, April 1911." Like so much ephemera, the exact reason for this inscription remains unknown, yet it is conceivable that a photo of David (or perhaps a very simple drawing) was once pasted to the cardboard as a gift to either his step-uncle Wilton Herriot and his wife Florence or James King, the only brother of Nellie Cushing, and that at a later date, Peter used the cardboard as backing for his painting. [5]

A strange coincidence related to Peter's birthday of May 26, 1913 takes us back some sixteen years to 1897, the year that Bram Stoker's Gothic masterpiece *Dracula* was published by Constable of London. For many years, Dracula scholars have hotly debated exactly when Stoker's novel first appeared on the shelves of booksellers in London. Some argue that it was between May 30 and June 24, due to an anonymous review in *The Athenaeum* for June 26, while others contend that the date is closer to the first week of June. However, even though Constable itself is not certain of the exact date, Elizabeth Miller of the *Journal of Dracula Studies* is convinced that May 26 is the accurate date of release.

By the age of five in 1918, Peter had discovered his latent talent for art which at first was expressed through what he calls pavement art or displaying his drawings propped up against the walls of a hallway and waiting with bated breath for his father to come home from Selby and Sanders to offer "a token of his appreciation" in the shape of a few spare pennies. [6] Peter was also a voracious reader and along with enjoying favorites like the *Gem* and *The Magnet*, his interest in "literature" expanded to include penny dreadfuls, a popular form of cheap and sensationalized fiction with lurid, full-color covers and "ballyhoo" stories aimed at middle-class young boys. Peter mentions his father having to pay two pence for *The Schoolboy's Own*

Library, published in London by the Amalgamated Press with titles like *The Island of Terror* with a cover depicting a cannibal lighting a fire beneath a half-naked young boy tied to a stake, and *The Schoolboy Crusoes* with another half-naked young boy being attacked by a giant, man-eating octopus. [7]

In addition to drawing and reading, Peter seems to have been fascinated with anything in miniature, especially Britains farm toys and model soldiers which he began collecting around the age of eight. These miniature lead figures were first produced in the early 1890s by toymaker William Britain (1828-1906); his oldest son, William Britain, Jr., is credited with inventing hollow casting for the production of toy soldiers, a totally new process that allowed the Britain miniature toy company to outpace its British and German competitors. Peter's fascination with miniatures continued into adulthood, and thanks to a newsreel film by British Pathé, dated December 11, 1956, we are allowed to witness Peter and his large collection of toy soldiers at his home in Kensington. In this newsreel, there are several master shots of Peter, surrounded by his precious books, meticulously hand-painting his soldiers as he compares them to several drawings for historical accuracy. Other shots show him arranging his soldiers and other figures on a battlefield laid across the floor, all according to rules designed by science-fiction master H.G. Wells in *Little Wars*, published in 1913, which outlines in detail how to play war games, a pastime that Wells himself often enjoyed using Britains miniature toy soldiers. [8]

At the age of ten or thereabouts, Peter had advanced into theatrics by staging his own productions at home in Dulwich, hoping to make a decent profit from his meager audience in order to have spending money. "I threw myself into intensive rehearsals," Peter recalls, "with my glove puppets" or Punch and Judy set of marionettes, made up of various characters like a doctor, a ghost, a policeman, a court jester, and even the devil. With Peter as the "professor" or puppeteer and David as his "bottler" or money collector, this version of a young boy's Grand Guignol culminated "in poor Punch hanging on the gibbet, whacked heartily by the policeman's truncheon, a somewhat macabre drama for the young." [9] Historically, Punch and Judy shows date back to the early 1600s and during the middle decades of the eighteenth century were commonly presented at taverns and outdoor festivities, such as Bartholomew Fair, the same locale where John Cushing produced *The Adventures of Sir Lubberly Lackbrains and His Man Blunderbuss* in April 1749, [10] a comedic play that quite certainly opened with a Punch and Judy show.

As a student at Purley County Grammar School in Croydon, circa 1923, Peter found it nearly impossible to concentrate on his schoolwork and often pleaded with his brother David for "assistance" with his homework, especially if the subject was mathematics. George Cushing certainly knew that Peter's academic abilities left much to be desired and that his wild imagination was the culprit for his failing grades. As Peter admits, his teachers at Purley quickly came to understand that teaching him was "futile and unrewarding" and that as a student, he was "a hopeless case." [11] However, one teacher in particular saw something special in Peter—the glimmerings of an actor with a passion for creativity and self-exploration. This was professor D.J. Davies, physics instructor who, as Peter acknowledges, "did much to foster my development" in the craft of acting, and instinctively knew that it was "a waste of his time and mine to attempt to instill my mind with any gems of scientific phenomena." So, instead of sitting in class, bored to death with talk of Robert Andrews Millikan's 1923 Nobel Prize award in physics for his research on electricity and the photoelectric effect, Peter was allowed to paint the scenery for a future stage presentation at Purley. [12]

For the next five years, Peter kept himself busy and rather contented by collecting cigarette cards, those "beautiful little mines of condensed information" on a whole range of subjects like animals, plants and flowers, antiquities, geography, and history. Also featured were famous personalities like William Gillette, the first actor to portray Sherlock Holmes; Sir Henry Irving, dignified and contemplative in black and white for Ogden's Guinea Gold cigarettes; and Ellen Terry as Marguerite in *Faust* for Players Past and Present full-color cigarette cards. He also discovered the excitement of exploring on foot and bicycle the "glorious surrounding countryside of Surrey" [13] with its lush, rolling hills and verdant meadows stretching as far as "Brighteyes" could see and the occasional tree-canopied road mottled by the browns and golds of autumn. In this breathtaking environment, Peter came to appreciate the wonders of the natural world about him and surely gazed adoringly at the beauty of the full moon during many late evening romps in the month of June with his brother David leading the way and most probably astray on many occasions.

As the old adage goes, "All things must pass" as did David Cushing from the household of his loving parents sometime in 1928 at the age of eighteen per the instructions of his father—"Go out and make a living for yourself, my son." Here is an echo from the past when circa 1898, Henry William Cushing told his son George that after he leaves school, "I shall endeavour to find you some kind of employment. After that, you can expect no further help from me." [14] Thus, with the possible assistance of his fellow Freemasons in the Lodge of Asaph and those mysterious "colleagues" at Carleton Chambers, Henry Cushing found suitable employment for George as a quantity surveyor with the firm of Selby and Sanders, established in 1899 in Tonbridge, Kent, and still in business today.

In effect, George Cushing did the same thing for David when he informed him that it was time to leave home and make his own mark in the world. Although David had at some point in his early youth decided to become a farmer (inklings of the old Cushing inclination for the agricultural life via Norfolk), George Cushing had other ideas and gradually convinced David to accept a position with an anonymous insurance company in London. According to Peter, his father used "his influence in securing the position," but when David grew restless working in a "brick and mortar" environment amid the noise and bustle of London, George "arranged" for David to set up a "small holding" or acreage of his own at Norwood Hill in Surrey. [15]

In 1933, when it was time to advise Peter to seek out his fortune away from the comforts of home, George Cushing once again used his influence to obtain a position for his youngest son in the Drawing Office of the Surveyor's Department at the Coulsdon and Purley Urban District Council. Of course, Peter had long desired to become an actor like his paternal grandfather Henry William Cushing, but this was conveniently snuffed out by George Cushing, at least for the meantime.

Exactly how George Cushing managed to "pull some strings" as Peter mentions is quite easy to explain, for like his father Henry William Cushing and step-uncle Wilton Herriot, George Cushing was a Freemason, a member of the Golden Fleece Lodge, no. 4739, in the city of London. Created on May 6, 1925, this lodge met at various places over the years, such as the Queens Hotel between 1925 and 1927; the London Masonic Centre for more than fifteen years; and finally at the Masonic Hall in Wolverton, where it currently operates. [16] Interestingly, the Golden Fleece Lodge held its fiftieth anniversary celebration in 1975 at Freemason's Hall, Great Queen Street, a familiar locale for Henry Cushing and his fellow Lodge of Asaph comrades.

As outlined in a search response from the Library and Museum of Freemasonry, dated February 1, 2011, George Cushing was initiated into the Golden Fleece Lodge on March 3, 1927, passed on June 2, and raised on September 1. However, for reasons that remain unexplained, he resigned his membership on December 18, 1934 when Peter was twenty-one years old. It should be noted that Peter was not a Freemason despite some spurious evidence to the contrary, such as the fact that the cake for his eightieth birthday in 1993 bore a center ornament in the shape of a six-pointed star (a hexagram) which can be found on the interior and exterior walls of most Masonic lodges; also, the woodwork of the bench at "Cushing's View" in Whitstable closely resembles one of the classic symbols of Freemasonry, the square and the compass, when viewed from the back. Another interesting item is that almost every Masonic lodge performs specific rites as plays or dramas on a stage with actors, costumes, lights, and sound. Therefore, during his seven-year tenure with the Golden Fleece Lodge, George Cushing as a "raised" member certainly participated in these performances, thus making him an actor of sorts.

As nothing more than a "glorified office boy" in the Drawing Office of the Surveyor's Department, twenty year-old Peter devoted almost all of his spare time to realizing his life-long ambition to become an actor. Thanks to what he calls a rota system that gave each employee of the company one Saturday morning off from work every month, Peter was able to make short excursions into London's West End, famous for its theatre districts, and once inside a particular venue, enjoy the "intoxicating atmosphere and heady odour" of the theatre, a conglomerate of "dust, distemper, and grease paint" amid the shadows and dimly-lit backstage corridors, some of which were purported to be haunted by the spirits of long-dead stage performers. [17]

Peter also maintained his relationship with professor and friend D.J. Davies by participating in school plays at Purley County Grammar School, along with amateur productions held at churches in Croydon, such as St. Mary's and St. Dominic's. However, because of his job at the offices of the Urban District Council, Peter was unable to properly study his lines and rehearse his roles, yet he did manage to convince his employers that the maps in the attic required "some semblance of order," thus allowing him to practice in this "private theatre, draped with cobwebs and with spiders and mice" among the paper relics of the past strewn about the floor and tucked in cubbyholes and dusty cabinets. [18]

Ironically, one of the periodicals that Peter bought and read on a weekly basis was *The Stage*, the foremost theatrical newspaper of the early 1930s and a virtual treasure trove for aspiring actors and actresses via its help wanted columns. Out of the hundreds of advertisements, Peter's attention was drawn to a typically narrow, rectangular box across the width of a column that read in so many words, "Wanted: juvenile character actor/assistant stage manager/scene painter, prepared to work all hours. A lazy bones won't last five minutes. No fancy prices" [19] (i.e., do not ask for much money). But unfortunately for Peter, most of these advertisements called for previous experience, a non-reference to amateur theatrical ventures at Purley and in the auditorium of a local church. In essence, no experience, no job.

But this did not discourage Peter from answering these types of help wanted ads with ill-conceived letters that always failed to mention his lack of experience. As might be suspected, after months of sending out letters to prospective employers, Peter did not receive any replies. He then came up with the idea of changing his surname, thinking this might increase his chances for employment. "I received a reply to one of my applications," he says, and with "trembling hands, I tore open the envelope." It appears that Ling was a very poor choice for a pseudonymous surname, due to the response, "I'm afraid there is limited scope for a Chinese actor in the repertory movement." [20] This type of predicament serves as an excellent example of Peter's determination and fortitude and symbolizes his perseverance in the face of defeat. It also illuminates how quickly Peter came to realize that the key to success was experience or hands-on field work that must be obtained by any means possible.

After a year of attempting to gain some kind of employment in professional theatre and not having any success whatsoever, Peter experienced his first bout of depression which is generally characterized by feelings of sadness, despair, and discouragement related to some type of personal loss, in this instance, Peter's inability to find employment in the theatre which would free him from the shackles of a lowly office boy at the Urban District Council. To make things worse, Peter was also quite upset over his father's apparent indifference to his watercolors and being told repeatedly that he was hopeless, a situation that many artists can certainly relate to when family members shrug off their talent as worthless and of no consequence.

Thus, at the age of twenty-one in 1934 and still living with his parents, Peter's great desire to become a full-fledged actor and "tread the boards" like his grandfather Henry William Cushing some forty years earlier partially faded away. "I became secretive and solitary," says Peter, "withdrawing deeper and deeper into my world of dreams, building around myself a protective carapace" [21] or an impenetrable barrier of self-imposed solitude. Peter's behavior during this difficult time in his life is typical of a person suffering from depression, such as avoiding family members, immersing oneself in daydreams and frivolous thoughts, and contemplating a permanent way out of reality.

One fateful day, Peter Cushing made up his mind to commit suicide. After placing a suicide note near a clock on the fireplace mantelpiece, he boarded a train for Exmouth, a popular resort spot in East Devon that buttresses the Atlantic Ocean, and upon arriving, headed for the two hundred foot high peak at Orcombe Point, "a good spot to drop off into oblivion." In his autobiography, Peter reveals his inner poet through a beautiful description of this serene locale:

It was a glorious day—cloudless, the sun sparkling on deep blue and emerald green waters . . . and so clear, I could see the sea bed of rippled sand and rocks, the clinging seawrack undulating in the gentle currents beneath the translucent surface. Overhead, gulls squawked raucously, (and) beneath my feet and all about me a profusion of nodding grass and soft cushions of thrift, bedecked with chalkhill blue butterflies basking in the warmth, and Six-Spot burnets flying their warning colors. [22]

But because of his fascination with the natural world and the distractions of a wheatear (a small, colorfully plumed bird indigenous to the "Old World" of Europe), Peter became lost in thought and soon found himself in the resort town of Budleigh Salterton, lying at the mouth of the River Otter and the birthplace of Sir Walter Raleigh. While drinking "a delicious Devonshire cream tea amongst the garden hollyhocks of a thatched cottage," [23] Peter must have thought of many things, such as his loving parents back home in Croydon; his brother David toiling away at his farm in Surrey; and perhaps even Mr. Davies scribbling nonsensical scientific formulas on a blackboard at Purley County Grammar School. Thoughts of suicide, however, dissipated, and Peter ended up on the train heading back home. Although he does not mention it, Peter must have walked in the door of his parent's home just in time to retrieve the suicide note on the mantelpiece and destroy it.

It was at this juncture in the life of Peter Cushing that destiny in the form of an unidentified periodical discarded by a fellow train passenger on a luggage rack stepped in and changed Peter's outlook on his seemingly miserable life forever. While glancing through this periodical, Peter came across an article that mentioned scholarships at the Guildhall School of Music and Drama, founded in 1880 and long considered as one of the finest conservatories dedicated to the performing arts in Europe. At first, Peter was a bit apprehensive about applying to this prestigious school, but whatever he said in his letter of application persuaded someone with influence to set up an interview. Upon arriving for the interview, Peter came face-to-face with Allan Aynesworth (1864-1959), a relatively obscure British actor of the late Victorian period, circa 1890, and best-known for his portrayal of Algernon Moncrieff in Oscar Wilde's highly successful stage parody *The Importance of Being Earnest*.

But as soon as Peter opened his mouth to speak, Aynesworth "clasped his hands to his ears and fell back in his chair." "Take him away!" he cried. "His voice offends me!" Peter was then given a second chance to meet with Aynesworth via his secretary, and when he entered not knowing what to expect, Aynesworth handed him a sheet of paper with various short phrases and said, "When you have mastered these basic vowel sounds, you may return—but not before." [24] Undaunted, Peter did exactly as Aynesworth had directed, and after several months of practice, he returned to Guildhall and was accepted as a freshman student. For Peter, this was a grand event, for it signaled some forward progression in his attempt to become a serious actor. As Peter puts it, "I felt I was at last making some headway toward my ultimate goal"—to stand on a real stage in front of a real audience and be accepted as a professional thespian, just like Henry Cushing and Wilton Herriot all those years ago in London. [25]

Peter's initiation into the life of a stage actor occurred in 1935 when he appeared in two plays at Guildhall, first as Ben Lorris in *The Red Umbrella*, a 1928 comedic fantasy by Brenda Girvin and Monica Cosens (ironically, a dialectical form of Cushing); and second, as Frederick Towers in George Kelly's *The Torch-Bearers*, a satirical comedy in three acts first produced on Broadway in 1922. However, in his autobiography, Peter mistakenly lends his character (the lead role, by the way) the surname of Towers when in fact it should be Ritter, at least according to the cast list in a copy of Kelly's play published by Samuel French of New York City in 1975.

Thinking that these two appearances at Guildhall might be sufficient enough stage experience, Peter sent out more applications for employment. His first line of attack was the Connaught Theatre in Worthing, West Sussex, sending one letter of application every three weeks. "After six months of intensive fire," writes Peter, "to my utter joy and amazement, they surrendered . . . requesting me to go down and see Mr. Bill Fraser." [26] As it turns out, William Simpson Fraser (1908-1987), a Scottish-born actor and mainly recognized for his roles in British TV and film between 1938 and the early 1980s, had one important thing in common with Peter Cushing—before becoming an actor, Fraser was a lowly bank clerk, much like Peter's "glorified office boy" position at the Urban District Council. [27]

When Fraser offered Peter a walk-on part in J.B. Priestley's *Cornelius* as a creditor, safely tucked away behind a group of other creditors as they enter an office, he was certain that his dream of becoming a professional actor had been fulfilled; unfortunately, after attempting to steal the spotlight as a walk-on without any lines, Peter ended up as an assistant stage manager at the Connaught Theatre. Thus, "in June of 1936, after almost five years of blood, toil, tears, and sweat," Peter Cushing "entered the ranks of the profession" of acting with a "fifty percent drop in salary," due to hastily quitting his job at the Urban District Council after receiving the reply from Fraser. [28]

Unlike so many individuals in the world of theatre and film, Peter Cushing was a teetotaler, a term generally used for an individual that does not consume alcohol under any circumstances because of moral and/or religious beliefs or simply because the taste of alcohol does not appeal to them. In his autobiography, Peter describes a party that was held after the showing of *Cornelius* at the Connaught Theatre in which he served "liquid refreshments" or hard liquor to those in attendance. "My knowledge of alcohol," declares Peter, "was limited, although I had observed its effects upon those who imbibed not wisely but too well." [29] Hours later, after only drinking tonic water, Peter was the only person at the party still able to stand up, making him the perfect escort for Mr. Fraser who obviously over-imbibed.

However, in his preface to Peter's second publishing venture with Weidenfeld and Nicolson in 1988, *Past Forgetting: Memoirs of the Hammer Years*, Peter Gray, Cushing's longtime friend and fellow actor, notes that after meeting Peter on a train bound for Nottingham to join Harry Hanson's Court Players, "Sandwiches were swopped and one of us had a Guinness which we shared," a reference to Guinness Stout, brewed and bottled in Ireland. Gray also adds that Helen Cushing often warmed up a Guinness Stout for her husband at home in Airlie Gardens where the Cushings lived during Peter's "lean years." [30] Obviously then, Peter abstained from drinking hard liquor and only drank Guinness and other beers (and perhaps wine and champagne) on special occasions or as a simple refreshment and certainly not to excess like his former employer Mr. Fraser.

Shortly after his disastrous attempt to stand out in a crowd of creditors through some rather silly antics in *Cornelius* at the Connaught Theatre, Peter was invited to join the acting company of Peter Coleman whose home stage was the Grand Theatre in Southampton. But once again, Peter was hired as an assistant stage manager, yet this time around was offered the opportunity to fill out numerous cameo roles whenever it was required. It was here at the Grand Theatre, circa the first months of 1938, that Peter met Doreen Lawrence, the juvenile female lead in many of the plays performed at the Grand. As Peter recalls:

We became good friends. She came to tea at my lodgings one day to run through a scene we had together and was horrified when she noticed the walls of my 'bed-sit' were oozing with moisture, and tiny fungi sprouting on the ceiling. The house possessed no bath, and the loo was at the bottom of a long, narrow garden. She lived with her parents in Southampton and they most kindly insisted I stay with them until I could find less damp and more convenient quarters to lay my weary head. [31]

Miss Lawrence is not mentioned by Peter in any other passages in his autobiography and does not provide any indication that his relationship with Miss Lawrence was more than just amiable. But in an article for "This England" magazine, Sam Brearley, a former member of the William Brookfield Players that Peter joined sometime in the spring of 1938, states that Miss Lawrence was Peter's girlfriend. [32] However, Doreen Lawrence (her stage name, born Doreen Mary Beadle in 1922), now writing under Doreen Hawkins, the wife of British actor Jack Hawkins from 1947 until his death in 1973, goes even further by declaring in her 2009 autobiography *Drury Lane to Dimapur: Wartime Adventures of an Actress* that she was briefly engaged to Peter sometime during his stint with the Brookfield Players.

As Hawkins explains it (seventy years after the fact), she was Peter's first true love interest, or rather, his first female obsession, and when George Cushing became aware of what was occurring, he quickly agreed to give Peter the funds for his "one-way trip" to Hollywood. Understandably, George Cushing was quite upset because Doreen Lawrence was only sixteen years old in 1938 and certainly did not want his twenty-five year-old son to become romantically involved with such a young girl. Hawkins also alleges that Peter made her feel uneasy, due to his "maternal instincts and expectations," meaning that Peter viewed her as a sort of mother replacement. [33]

Also, it seems rather odd that Miss Lawrence's parents would allow Peter to stay at their home in Southampton knowing that he was nine years older than their daughter, unless of course they had already agreed to their marriage in line with British law that mandates parental consent for a sixteen year-old female. If all of this is true, then it contradicts Peter's admission that despite falling "in and out of love with practically every young lady" he happened to be working with, the time to pursue these "romances" simply did not exist. [34] Although this alleged close relationship between Peter and Miss Lawrence was not in any way scandalous, it certainly illustrates Peter's need for female companionship as a vibrant and somewhat naive young man.

In mid 1938, via the assistance of his "old stand-by" *The Stage*, Peter was invited to join what he calls an "elite society" known as Harry Hanson's Court Players, a popular repertory company based in the borough of Hastings in East Sussex and not to distant from Budleigh Salterton, where Peter thought of throwing himself off the cliff at Orcombe Point in 1934. As manager and proprietor, the always clever and industrious Harry Hanson purchased the rights to successful plays from London's West End theatre district in order to present them at Hastings Pier and other venues throughout England, such as the Theatre Royal in Nottingham in the East Midlands, the Princes Theatre in Bradford in West Yorkshire, and the Grand Theatre in Swansea, Wales. A prime example of Hanson's industriousness, or perhaps his penchant for recycling, is that "it was not unusual to see a red chintz (flower patterned) table cloth used as curtains" or to have the stage carpenter straighten out used nails rather than buy new ones for backdrops and panels. One of Hanson's many eccentricities was to wear a different colored hair piece for each season of the Court Players and anecdotally, he allegedly wore a white hair piece during the player's presentation of *Dracula* in the early 1940s and quipped, "My dears, you have played your parts so well that my hair has turned white with fright!" [35]

Thanks to *The Stage* archives, two specific plays in which Peter appeared as a member of the Court Players can now be brought to light. In mid July of 1938, at the Theatre Royal in Nottingham, Peter received ninth billing in "Double Door," a suspenseful melodrama by Elizabeth MacFadden and based on the 1934 film version. As one of the roving theatre correspondents for *The Stage* reports, the Court Players gave an "acceptable performance of an engrossing and thrilling play" featuring the "autocratic and domineering" Victoria Van Brett who locks her naive sister Caroline in a vault along with the family's treasured heirlooms and then tries to do the same to her half-brother's new bride, Ann Darrow. Of course, Victoria is the only person in the Van Brett family that possesses the combination to the vault. Peter's role in this play is not mentioned, but along with other lesser character actors, his performance is noted as more than adequate. [36] In late August, 1938, Peter appeared in "Count Your Chickens," also at the Theatre Royal in Nottingham and the nineteenth production by Harry Hanson and his Court Players. This comedic vehicle "offers a cleverly studied impersonation of the romantic gigolo" and the women that end up as his sexual conquests and features Peter in an unidentified role which the correspondent for *The Stage* notes as being a "clever characterization." [37]

While a member of Harry Hanson's Court Players, Peter became acquainted with Peter Gray who turned out to be a "marvelous companion" with an avid interest in literature and the arts. One writer in particular that appealed to Gray's wide-ranging interest in British literature of the early twentieth century was J.B. Priestley whose work Peter Cushing had been introduced to via Mr. Fraser through the play *Cornelius*. As a playwright and writer of fiction and non-fiction titles, John Boynton Priestley, born in Yorkshire in 1894 and the son of a schoolmaster, was extremely prolific with over forty plays, thirty novels, and other books on subjects as varied as poet Thomas Love Peacock, Charles Dickens, England's involvement in World War II, Queen Victoria, and the reign of the Edwardian monarchy. During the early 1930s, a number of Priestley's novels were adapted for the screen with perhaps the most widely-recognized being *The Old Dark House* (1932), based on his novel *Benighted* (1927) and directed by James Whale with Boris Karloff as Morgan, a brutish and often drunk mute butler of the Femms, and Melvyn Douglas as a fatalistic World War I veteran of the trenches.

As an actor with Harry Hanson's Court Players, Peter Gray received a number of sterling reviews from theatre critics for his work in plays alongside Peter Cushing, such as "Double Door" in which he appeared as the "eager and loyal young husband" of Ann Darrow, and "Count Your Chickens" as the "chivalrous young Stephen Harrington." [38] As a human being, Gray seems to have been especially likable, for Peter Cushing's mother Nellie "adored him" and was pleased that her son had found such an excellent companion. It also appears that Gray was deeply devoted to his wife Daphne Newton, for after her death in January of 1986, Gray became despondent with episodes of depression and solitude, similar in nature to Peter Cushing's initial reaction to his beloved Helen's death in 1971.

On the morning of September 30, 1938, British Prime Minister Neville Chamberlain landed at Heston Aerodrome just outside of London, and after stepping off the plane addressed a huge crowd of reporters with some much-needed good news concerning Adolf Hitler and his military advances in Eastern Europe. In his hand was a piece of paper signed by Hitler that outlined the terms of the Munich Agreement which many Britons felt was nothing short of appeasement to Hitler's demands to seize the Sudentenland, an area of Czechoslovakia largely populated by persons of German descent. Chamberlain's speech at the Aerodrome was positively received by the crowd gathered about him, particularly when he announced that peace had been achieved "with honor in our time."

Chamberlain's famous appeasement speech at the Aerodrome was also broadcast throughout Great Britain with thousands glued to their wireless radios, comfortable in the fact that Chamberlain had accomplished the impossible by preventing full-scale war with Hitler's Germany. As Peter describes this historic event, he had seen newsreels at the cinema of Chamberlain "holding up that famous, or in light of what was to come, infamous piece of paper" at the Heston Aerodrome. And like so many other fellow Britons, "In my ignorance, I took (Chamberlain's) word for it, and got on with the job at hand," [39] namely, the continuation of his flowering career as a stage actor.

Less than three months later, Peter acted upon a long-held dream by purchasing (with the assistance of his father) a "one-way" ticket to Hollywood, California, where the film industry was at its height during what many refer to as its Golden Age. Thus, at the age of twenty-five and with "high hopes and the abounding impetuosity of youth," [40] Peter left England for the first time in his life aboard the SS Champlain, bound for the United States and the great unknown.

After his arrival in New York City some ten days later, Peter put into action his "plan of campaign" that included visiting as many film production companies in the city as possible in seven days, seeking out some form of assistance or letters of introduction to studio casting directors in Hollywood. While tramping through the "Great White Way" or Broadway, as Peter recounts, he happened upon Walter Larney Goodkind (1909-2003), a versatile New York City-based talent agent for Universal and Columbia Pictures during the late 1920s and throughout the 1930s and a personal manager, literary agent, and part-time actor on Broadway in Tapestry in Grey in 1935. [41] It was Goodkind who furnished Peter with a letter of introduction to Edward Small Productions, owned and operated by United Artists producer Edward Small who began his career in Hollywood in 1924 as an independent film producer and promoter. This letter of introduction was most certainly handwritten by Goodkind, due to the complete absence of a typewritten or mimeographed copy in his personal business files, currently held by his grandson.

Exactly what Goodkind wrote in this letter of introduction remains unknown, but he must have said enough to get Peter past the gates of Edward Small Productions. "That I should turn up at this precise moment," recalls Peter, "was one of those extraordinary lucky breaks which we all need at some time or other during this life, but don't always get." [42] Once admitted to Edward Small studios, Peter was sent to see the casting director who quickly hired him for a small role as the King's Messenger in *The Man in the Iron Mask*, based on the historical romance novel by Alexandre Dumas, a role not unlike that of Henry William Cushing as a Citizen in Sir Henry Irving's 1894 production of *Faust*. It was through his participation in this 1939 film that Peter became acquainted with perhaps the greatest horror film director of all time—James Whale, "lean, tall, and sardonic," whose artistic career began in a prisoner of war camp in Holzminden, Germany, during World War I, where he acted in plays produced by his fellow camp inmates. Later on, Whale acted in a number of plays in London and worked as a part-time scenic designer, the perfect job for Whale whose artistic talents extended far beyond directing and producing. [43]

Of course, Whale is best remembered for *Frankenstein* (1931), a Universal project that allowed him to "dabble in the macabre" and perhaps pull Universal out of possible bankruptcy. According to Gregory William Mank, Carl Laemmle, Jr. failed to recognize in Whale during a meeting in June of 1931 "a man whose egomania, homosexuality, and drinking would eventually result in his exile" from Universal studios, or as a person "fated for a sordid death" [44] in his own swimming pool on May 29, 1957, less than four weeks after the release of Hammer's *Curse of Frankenstein* in Great Britain on May 2 and only three days after Peter's forty-fourth birthday.

Peter's Hollywood "career" was of short duration, lasting less than two full years from February 1939 to January 1941, and although he did appear in several important films alongside the likes of Carole Lombard, Louis Hayward, and Laurel and Hardy, and was directed by George Stevens, Peter's acting-related adventures in the hedonistic culture of Hollywood did not substantially affect his career, nor did it bring him popular recognition as a professional actor. In effect, Peter's self-imposed odyssey in Hollywood was a training ground for what was to come as a respected and admired stage, television, and film performer in his beloved England.

Shortly after wrapping up his acting duties in the Laurel and Hardy vehicle *A Chump at Oxford* sometime around September 1939, Peter was invited to a cricket party at the spacious home of Sir C. Aubrey Smith, a prominent British actor regarded by film historians as the "commander" of the Hollywood Raj, a tightly-knit coterie of English actors that invaded Hollywood in the late 1920s and 1930s in an attempt (which certainly succeeded) to infiltrate the American film industry. However, this was not the first invasion by the British in Hollywood, for in 1882, none other than Richard D'Oyly Carte, the theatrical manager and employer of William Penley and Florence Marryat, presented the play *Patience* in Hollywood and in the greater Los Angeles area after a successful and profitable run in London a year earlier. Incidentally, *Patience* was written by the theatrical partner of Arthur Sullivan, W.S. Gilbert, who wrote the one-act, operatic drama *Trial by Jury* with Penley in the role of the jury foreman. [45]

Some of the more prominent members of this British clique of actors included Nigel Bruce (Dr. Watson); Claude Rains (Whale's *The Invisible Man*); David Niven (*Old Dracula* with Hammer stars Linda Hayden, Veronica Carlson, and Freddie Jones) and George Sanders (*The Picture of Dorian Gray*). Two other members of this group are of special importance— Basil Rathbone and William Henry Pratt, a.k.a. Boris Karloff. This is an excellent example of foreshadowing in Peter's life as an actor with the above-mentioned cricket party thrown by C. Aubrey Smith as the locale for his encounter with Rathbone, considered by many as the quintessential Sherlock Holmes, and Karloff whose acting career went into overdrive after appearing as the monster in Whale's seminal horror classic *Frankenstein*.

Thus, although not officially recognized as a standing member of C. Aubrey Smith's Hollywood Raj group, Peter certainly fits the bill as a self-exiled British actor, especially if we consider the possibility that he was fully aware of the so-called "British Invasion" before leaving England for the United States in early 1939. If this is accurate, then Peter possessed yet another personal trait that served him extremely well as an actor—serendipity, or being in the right place at the right moment and knowing how to take full advantage of the situation at hand.

With his Hollywood adventures behind him, Peter returned to New York City in early January of 1941, the first stop in his "pilgrimage" to reach Great Britain by any means possible. Since his finances were insufficient to pay for a "one-way ticket" back to England, Peter sought out employment and managed to secure a number of acting positions to help pay for the continuation of his "pilgrimage" home. After a year in New York City, Peter boarded "the Iron Horse north-bound for Canada" [46] on February 8, 1942, ending up in the city of Montreal, where he obtained employment as a theatre usher at Lowes State Cinema. To pass the idle hours between ushering at the movie house, Peter resorted to one of his favorite hobbies—building miniature replicas, this time a Bechstein or a grand piano manufactured originally in Berlin, Germany by the C. Bechstein Pianofortefabrik Company. Ironically, C. Bechstein was the official piano maker for the monarchy of Russia during the reign of the doomed Czar Nicholas II whose personal manifesto to his Russian subjects concerning individual freedom and civil liberties was annulled by government officials on October 17, 1905, seven months after the birth of Violet Helene Beck, the future wife of Peter Cushing.

In March 1942, Peter left Montreal and traveled by train to Halifax, the capital city of Nova Scotia. It was here in this freezing maritime environment, highlighted by Halifax Harbour, the final resting place for numerous World War II ships and German U-boats, that Peter's "pilgrimage" to England was about to conclude aboard what he calls a "banana ship of the Fyffe and Elder line," [47] a major shipping company established in London in 1901 and primarily known during the early 1940s as a supplier of bananas and other tropical fruit from the Caribbean basin. Apparently, Peter was unsure of the ship's final destination or port of call and assumed that his first sighting of the shores of England would be the White Cliffs of Dover jutting out into the Straits of Dover and the English Channel. However, Peter figured wrongly, for his "pilgrimage" concluded in the city of Liverpool at the head of the River Mersey in northwestern England some one hundred and fifty miles north of London.

Thus, after almost fifteen months of traveling, Peter was back at home in England. His long journey, spanning almost seven thousand miles, was finally over. It would not be too much of a strain on the imagination to compare Peter to the tragic Greek hero Odysseus, the sacker of the windy city of Troy who cursed the Gods and spent ten years wandering the wine-dark seas of the Aegean in an attempt to return home to Ithaca, where his beloved wife Penelope unwove a tapestry every night as a way of fending off her many suitors, and gazed longingly out to sea for her long-lost husband. Little did Peter realize that his Penelope was patiently waiting in the wings for the first curtain of the night to rise on a new dramatic play that would last for twenty-eight years.

§

4

Helen:
The Poetry
of her Presence

In the early spring of 1824, fifteen year-old Edgar Poe, then living in the city of Richmond, Virginia, with his foster parents John and Francis Allan, paid a short visit to the home of a friend just down the street from Allan's spacious Moldavia estate on the corner of Fifth and Main. Upon entering the parlor, Edgar was introduced to Jane Craig Stanard, the mother of his friend and at least ten years older than him, a rather striking, dark-haired woman with a love for poetry and the romantic verses of Lord Byron and Percy Shelley. As Poe scholar Arthur Hobson Quinn relates, "There seems to have been born between them an instant bond of sympathy which produced a deep effect" upon young Edgar. [1] Many years later, Poe recalled in a letter that Mrs. Stanard was "the first, purely ideal love of my soul," [2] a love without bounds, selfless and pure in heart.

Shortly after this visit, Jane Stanard died from a possible brain tumor, and young Edgar, being the poet that he was, took pen to paper and composed the following poem "To Helen" in honor of his first "ideal love":

> Helen, thy beauty is to me
> Like those Nicean barks of yore,
> That gently, o'er a perfumed sea,
> The weary, wayworn wanderer bore
> To his own native shore.
> On desperate seas long wont to roam,
> Thy hyacinth hair, thy classic face,
> Thy Naiad airs have brought me home

To the glory that was Greece
And the grandeur that was Rome.
Lo! in yon brilliant window-niche
How statue-like I see thee stand,
The agate lamp within thy hand!
Ah, Psyche, from the regions which
Are Holy Land! [3]

After the premature death of Jane Stanard, Poe became melancholy and depressed and is rumored to have paid nightly visits to the grave of his "Helen" in an attempt to quell his longings to be with her once again. But since Edgar was only fifteen years old at the time of Mrs. Stanard's death, he eventually overcame his depression and returned to a semblance of reality which unfortunately was not to last.

****

Following his arrival in England, Peter Cushing boarded another train via the historic town of Reigate in Surrey, where actor Melvyn Hayes, the young Victor in Hammer's *Curse of Frankenstein*, once lived on Glovers Road. In his autobiography, Peter describes in exquisite detail the countryside of Surrey as seen through the train window, the "panorama of our beautiful Shires" unfolding before him. This is also another fine specimen of Peter's poetic voice:

Neat hedgerows, skeletal trees sparkling with rime and black with rooks cawing noisily amongst their nests; ploughed fields and pasture land, revealing patches of verdant grass where the snow had melted, studded with cattle and sheep gently grazing besides meandering rivers and streams. [4]

Several days after almost giving his dear mother a heart attack when he unexpectedly showed up at David Cushing's farm in Surrey, Peter obtained employment with the Entertainments National Services Association which in the early 1940s at the height of World War II was controlled by the Ministry of Labour and National Service for the sole purpose of providing entertainment to British military personnel. By sheer coincidence, the headquarters for ENSA in London was the Theatre Royal in Drury Lane, the same venue once managed by James Henry Mapleson and where William Penley performed in *Charley's Aunt* in the early 1890s. It was just outside of this historic theatre in May 1942 that Peter first encountered Helen Beck, a meeting which later proved that "Fate's guiding hand was drawing her strings ever tighter," and like so many instances in his past was "another case of being in the right place at the right moment." [5]

As quoted in Peter's autobiography, when Helen first caught sight of her future husband, she quickly sensed that their paths had crossed at some point long ago. As Helen tells it,

Peter was "tall and lean (with) a pale, almost haggard face with astonishingly large blue eyes. On his head was an old, grey velvet hat, with a hole between the dents of its crown." His jacket was "beyond description and repair" and his spotless white shirt was "frayed at the cuffs and collar." Yet despite this outwardly appearance, "There was an aura about this beloved vagabond" who surely was a musician or an artist, due to his hands resembling those rendered by Albrecht Durer in his self-portrait of 1500. "I knew," admitted Helen, "I would love him for the rest of my days, and beyond." [6]

The familial ancestry of Helen Cushing is quite different from that of her husband; however, and this should come as no surprise, artistically-inclined relatives like Peter's step-uncles Albert Walter Cushing and Wilton Herriot are also found in Helen's lineage. The main difference lies in Peter's ancestral rural background in Norfolk and Helen's Russian pedigree, dating back to the days of Peter the Great, czar of Russia from 1682 to 1725. Helen's father, Ernest Beck, was born in St. Petersburg on May 5, 1875 (d. in London, November, 1950), and as a child relocated with his parents to Lancashire, England, where Ernest later became the proprietor of the James Beck Spinning Company, a maker of fine cloth and yarn products. Her mother, Helene Alexandra Fatima Enckell, was also born in St. Petersburg on June 19, 1879 (d. Amersham, Buckshire, England, May 14, 1951) with a Finnish background which helps to explain the marriage of Ernest and Helene in Hamina, Finland, on March 30, 1901. [7]

This marriage produced five children—Reginald Ernest (b. 1902); Godfrey Charles (b. 1903); Violet Helene (b. 1905); Elisabeth Marjorie (b. 1908); and Rosalind Doris "Rosita" (b. 1910), all born in St. Petersburg. [8] The oldest son Reginald became a film editor and worked alongside director Joseph Losey for *Don Giovanni* (1979), based on the opera by Mozart, and *A Doll's House* (1973), adapted from Henrik Ibsen's play and starring Jane Fonda. With the exception of Helen, the other Beck children apparently led completely normal lives with careers as varied as a merchant broker and a city librarian.

It is with Helen's grandparents that her familial ancestry turns especially fascinating. On the paternal side, Helen's grandfather, Carl Enckell, born in Helsinki, Finland on October 22, 1839 (d. Finland, February, 1921) was a general in the Imperial Russian army and later in life became the director of the Finland Cadet School in Hamina, originally founded in 1780. At the age of thirty-eight, Carl was assigned as the Chief of Staff of the Third Russian Infantry Division and fully participated in the Turkish wars from 1877 to 1878 in which he was wounded in the leg. He also seems to have had an interest in writing, due to keeping extensive journals on his military career, published as memoirs in 1990. [9] Helen's paternal grandmother (Carl's wife) was born in St. Petersburg on December 20, 1850 (d. Helsinki, Finland, August, 1923) as Helene Natalia Bronikowsky, a proper Polish baroness and the daughter of Maria Charlotta Adelheid who was related through marriage to the imperial and royal family of Austria-Hungary and the royal families of Liechtenstein in the early 1800s, thus making Helen Cushing a long-distance princess and baroness. [10]

Peter and Helen lived together under the same roof for almost an entire year after their chance meeting outside of the Theatre Royal. This indicates that Peter and Helen were quite broad-minded and saw nothing inappropriate about sharing not only the same residence but also the same bed or perhaps separate beds since Peter did admit several times that his relationship with Helen was more spiritual than sexual. "From its beginning," he relates, "our relationship had been unique, as though we were continuing something that had begun in another age. It was a spiritual union, the physical element holding little importance." In essence then, the foundation of Peter and Helen's long-term relationship was a "mutual desire to spend the rest of time together," not only in this life but also in the next. [11]

As a kind of reinforcement, when Peter realized that Helen like himself held a deep and abiding love for literature, ranging from Victor Hugo, the quintessential master of French Romanticism, to August Wilhelm Schlegel, poet and doyen of German Romanticism (with Russian giants Tolstoy and Chekhov thrown in for good measure), the drawstrings of the hands of Fate tightened like an ever-diminishing circle, ensuring that the relationship between these two unique individuals, not too far removed from the days of "rogues and vagabonds" during the late nineteenth century, would remain inviolate and permanent.

However, one unfortunate realization for Peter was that Helen's health was far from good, due to problems related to her inability to have children and recurrent respiratory disorders. According to Peter, during the first five months of their relationship, "I had become acutely aware" of Helen's painful coughing, and one evening during an "uncontrollable spasm," he noticed spots of blood on her handkerchief, a sure sign of emphysema or something far worse. In fact, on this particular evening, Helen was diagnosed as having experienced a hemorrhage which turned out to be Peter's first indication that Helen's health was precarious and skirted the thin line between wellness and incapacitation. [12] Ironically, almost the exact same circumstances upset Edgar Poe's marriage to his first cousin Virginia Eliza Clemm who one day suffered a hemorrhage while singing, a sure sign of consumption or tuberculosis which inevitably led to her death at the age of twenty-four in 1847.

Although there is no evidence to support the idea that Helen Cushing, often described as a petite woman with blonde hair and blue eyes, was somewhat telepathic or perhaps gifted with a strong sense of *déjà vu*, it appears from Peter's account that sometime before World War II, Helen became seriously ill in the city of Ashton-under-Lyne in Manchester which holds an annual celebration called the Black Knight pageant, based on the life of an English tyrant from the fifteenth century. Racked with delirium and hallucinations, Helen allegedly saw the "Angel of Death" and cried out that she was not ready to depart this world because "there is something left for me to do," namely, to act as the guiding and loving spirit for her dear Peter who certainly needed as much help as possible because of his shyness and introverted personality. [13]

Peter also relates that Helen told him just before their marriage on April 10, 1943 at the District of Kensington Office of the Registrar, that the "Angel of Death" had spared her life so she could look after him and tend to his needs and wants. She also hinted at a premonition of her premature death, telling Peter that he "must be free" and not feel as if possessed or trapped. "I shall always be there when you need me," she said, an obvious reference to being "there" in spirit but not in body. [14]

When Helen Cushing gave up her own stage career to become Peter's greatest advocate and advisor on all things related to the profession of acting, their lives together as a team from about 1943 to 1959 yielded a number of successes. All of the quotes and reviews that follow have been taken from *The Stage*, Peter's original source for his first acting job while working as a "glorified office boy" for the Coulsdon and Purley Urban District Council. Some of the plays discussed in these reviews might be new to some readers, while others have been covered in other books, especially Gullo's 2004 biography. But what makes these reviews so interesting is the subjective commentary of the reporters, most of whom had never heard of Peter Cushing prior to 1948.

For Richard Brinsley Sheridan's *The Rivals*, presented at the Criterion Theatre in late September of 1945 as a "comedy of British manners in five acts," Peter's character of the fatuous Faulkland was "played with great care and a careful sense of style" as contrasted with Captain Absolute, played by Anthony Quayle who was always "too mannered to be wholly satisfying as a romantic figure." This particular performance at the Criterion also featured Michael Gough in a "good character study as the eminent gentleman's gentleman" or servant to Captain Absolute. [15] It should be noted that Gough's acting heritage dates back even further than that of his good friend Peter Cushing, due to a certain Robert Gough who first appeared on the English stage in 1592 in mostly female parts which was not an uncommon occurrence; he is also mentioned as ranking at number twenty-three in the actor's list in the Shakespearean folio of 1623. [16]

In late November of 1946 at the "Q" Theatre, J. Lee Thompson's *The Curious Dr. Robson* featured Peter in the title role as (of all things) a slightly mad doctor with "abnormal habits." A portion of the review for this three-act play deserves to be recorded because of the uncanny resemblance of its scenario to a series of films made by Hammer with Peter as the main attraction:

Following in the footsteps of the amazing Dr. Clitterhouse comes a curious Dr. Robson, another member of the medical profession with abnormal habits. Curious he is indeed and becomes more so as each scene unfolds. This play is described as a comedy thriller. The early scenes contain most of the comedy, but after the occasion of the first murder, this element is neglected in favor of the thrilling aspect. It is a pity that the chief purveyor of comedy is the first victim of the killer . . . However, for those with a taste for the grim, there are two charmingly arranged murders. The murderer's identity is revealed quite early on, but the tension is well-maintained until the final curtain. Dr. Robson is a gentleman with a taste for severing girl's heads from their bodies and extracting their brains for some sort of experimental work and manages quite successfully offstage to dispose of four victims and in view of the audience, and another two before he is disturbed and compelled to commit suicide as he is about to finish off his wife. As Robson, Cushing has a strong and emotional character to depict, and although not quite the type one would associate with this part, he puts up a very good performance with a very strong final scene that is quite effective. [17]

In early 1948, Peter was hired by Laurence Olivier to appear in his long-awaited film adaptation of Shakespeare's immortal classic *Hamlet* as Osric, often described by Shakespearean scholars as a *boulevardier*, a man of noble birth yet roguish in his habits who frequents taverns and places of ill-repute in search of distractions from reality and of course much food and drink. The character of Osric also functions as a sort of comedic respite from all of the dramatic action in the play.

Peter's film role as Osric has a very strange connection with another version of Shakespeare's play performed some two hundred years earlier in 1750 with John Cushing at Covent Garden in the role of Osric, a smirking villain responsible for dipping a rapier in a cup of poison and handing it to Laertes so as to kill Hamlet with a single cold thrust to the heart. What makes this so unnerving is that the character list for *Hamlet* contains seventeen major and minor male roles. How then did John Cushing and Peter end up playing the exact same character when Olivier could have easily assigned another role to Peter?

As a result of Peter's splendid performance in the film version of *Hamlet*, Olivier invited him to join the rest of the cast (thirty-eight in total) in an extended 1948 tour of Australia and New Zealand. However, Peter would only agree to this if Helen were allowed to accompany him. "There were enough separations during the war," replied Olivier after Peter made it clear that he did not wish to leave Helen behind, due in part to her deteriorating health. "Of course, your Helen shall be one of us," and with that, Peter and Helen boarded a ship in Liverpool and departed to the wilds of Australia. [18] Five weeks later, the balmy shores of Western Australia came into view off the ship's bow, and not too far inland stood the city of Fremantle. Unknown to Peter, he was now less than thirty miles from the resort town of Cottesloe, where Albert Walter Cushing was living in 1910 at the "White House" on Warton Street. Whether Uncle "Bertie" was alive and well in 1948 remains to be seen, for his obituary has never been located. But Peter certainly did think about his long-lost and banished step-uncle, for he mentions that "In all those past months" while touring Australia, "I never caught sight of wandering uncle Bertie" who would have been seventy-nine years old in 1948. [19]

In mid January of 1949, Laurence Olivier and his Old Vic Theatre Company presented at the New Theatre in London an adaptation of Richard Brinsley Sheridan's comedy *The School for Scandal*, a "magnificent production that brought together a highly-talent company," composed of Olivier, Vivien Leigh, Peter Cushing (as Joseph Surface) and Derrick Penley, the grandson of William Sydney Penley of *Charley's Aunt*. As for Peter, his part in this play is described as being "in the familiar traditional vein of suave and polished hypocrisy" or a person of nobility in eighteenth century France living an extravagant lifestyle while others suffer and starve in abject poverty. [20] Through the inclusion of Derrick Penley in the cast for this play directed by Olivier, Peter came full circle by performing on the same stage with the grandson of William Penley, perhaps the closest friend and confidant of Henry William Cushing.

Less than one month later, Peter returned to the New Theatre in a revival of Shakespeare's *Richard III*. As an unidentified correspondent for *The Stage* reports, "As a tragic actor, Sir Laurence Olivier achieves greatness" in this production as "an utter villain, even perhaps a degree more villainous than Shakespeare intended." Thus, Olivier's portrayal of King Richard "makes the character a completely sinister, malignant figure," much in line with Sir Henry Irving's portrayal of the doomed Plantagenet monarch during the fifth American tour of 1896. [21] In this particular production, Peter acted as the Duke of Clarence, yet in other *Richard III* productions (i.e., in Australia) headed by Olivier, he also played the role of Cardinal Bouchier, the same character performed by Henry William Cushing in 1897 at the Lyceum Theatre. Once again, with more than twenty major and minor male roles within the cast list for *Richard III*, it seems very odd that Peter ended up playing the exact same part as his grandfather.

Three additional plays deserve some notice—*The Gay Invalid*, presented at the Opera House in Manchester on November 6, 1950 with Peter in the title role as Valentine and Derrick Penley as Potion; and *The Silver Whistle* at the Duchess Theatre in London on May 1, 1956 with Peter as Oliver Erwenter and Ernest Thesiger (Dr. Praetorius in *The Bride of Frankenstein*) as Mr. Beebe. Peter's performance in this play as "the strange god from the machine who so swiftly changes the lives of those upon whom he descends," is described as "excessively boisterous" yet filled with "enormous zest." [22] Lastly, *The Sound of Murder* at the Aldwych Theatre in London on August 5, 1959 with Peter in the lead role as Charles Norbury, a "suitably detestable" character and the intended victim of a murder plot gone awry. [23]

In essence, if it was not for Helen's unconditional support and devotion, Peter's acting career just might have ended in the middle years of the 1940s, leaving him as he put it, "A failure at forty" in 1953. As an example, shortly after the death of Helen's father in 1950, Peter seriously considered returning to repertory theatre to help with their financial problems, but Helen thought otherwise and bought a copy of *Radio Times* which listed available positions in British television and other media. She then sat down and typed out a whole slew of letters to TV producers, leaving enough space at the bottom for Peter to sign. "I wasn't very sanguine about this," admits Peter, due to believing that no one associated with the relatively new medium of television had ever heard of him. However, offers started pouring in, and Peter quickly found himself in high demand as an actor for the only TV channel in Great Britain, the all-powerful and monopolistic British Broadcasting Corporation. [24]

Some weeks later, Helen entered St. George's Hospital for a hernia operation and after having surgery remarked that her stomach "was beginning to look like an aerial view of a railway terminus," or a mass of stitches. This was during one of Peter's "dry spells" as an actor, so he turned to his aging father for financial assistance. Just before giving Peter a check, George Cushing asked his son, perhaps out of a concern that Peter might be back for more assistance, "Why don't you get some other job to do when you are disengaged, like your grandfather?" This simple question confirms the previous suggestion that Henry Cushing worked at other jobs during his own "dry spells" as an opera singer for Mapleson and as an actor for Sir Henry Irving. George Cushing also mentions a "front-of-house manager" [25] or a person that supervises all of the activity related to managing and operating areas of the theatre open to the public, such as the seating sections, the front lobby, and the foyer bar. Thus, did Henry Cushing work during his "dry spells" as a "front-of-house manager" at the Lyceum Theatre as George Cushing seems to be inferring?

Helen was also an avid admirer of Peter's talent as a painter and told him many times over the years that he should pursue this "hobby" with much more vigor and intensity. Obviously, someone besides Helen was greatly interested in Peter's thirty year-long avocation as a painter because on December 5, 1958, some six months after appearing in Hammer's *The Revenge of Frankenstein*, a special exhibition of his watercolors was held at the London-based gallery of the Fine Arts Society, located at 148 Bond Street and established as a major art gallery in 1876. An unidentified critic for *The Stage* writes that this exhibition revealed "this talented actor to be no less notable as a painter," and then describes in some detail Peter's methodology and style:

In watercolor, Cushing has selected a difficult and under-appreciated medium which he handles in a clean, decisive, and technically proficient manner. His method of using the white paper itself as the lightest color in his range is in the best watercolor tradition. He has specialized almost exclusively in the English landscape, and if, en masse, the cool tones of his pictures make the exhibition seem slightly monotonous in comparison with the interest and beauty of each picture individually, this is only due to the similarity of his subject matter. Two flower paintings, notably one of syringa, prove him a master of this seldom satisfactory subject. [26]

As a serious painter, Peter's main influence related to his style, methodology, and iconography was Edward Seago, born in the county of Norfolk (Peter's ancestral home) in 1910. As a child, Seago was plagued by a number of recurring illnesses and as a result spent a good deal of his non-study time in his bedroom sketching views through a window. However, his parents did not approve of his artistic endeavors and attempted to "convince him that a career in business was a better course to follow" (intimations of George Cushing trying to dissuade Peter from the life of an actor). In the early 1930s, Seago was "discovered" by Henry Mond, the second Lord Melchett, who became his most ardent supporter and patron. Interestingly, at one of Lord Melchett's elegant dinner parties, Seago met H.G. Wells, the author of Peter's tactical war game manuals, and George Bernard Shaw who once quipped that artists sacrifice everything for their art, and when the art is acting (as well as painting), it is the self that becomes body and soul. [27]

Some of Peter's finest watercolors were rendered in the mid to late 1950s when he could afford high-quality painting supplies because of his extensive film and TV work. A few of the most well-known of these watercolors includes "View of Whitstable Harbor" (ca. 1958); "Norfolk Landscape, after Edward Seago" (1955); "Brenley Corner, Kent" (1957); and "First Signs of Autumn, Trimingham, Norfolk" (ca. 1955), an iconic wooded country scene very much in line with Seago's landscapes of his native Norfolk with Trimingham lying not too distant northward from Wymondham, the birthplace of Peter's great-great-grandfather John Cushing. Although Seago was mostly a self-taught artist, Peter did attend the Croydon School of Art, circa 1931, which aided in stimulating his need to create something out of nothing.

Throughout the years of the 1950s, Helen Cushing's health see-sawed between wellness and vitality, sickness and morbidity. In 1952, Peter decided to leave Helen at home while appearing in the play *The Wedding Ring* at various locales in and around London and the provinces, but his thoughts always drifted back to her, particularly while observing through a train window "the beautiful and varied countryside" of the "Shires," "bathed in August sunshine." Peter also describes the weather in Lancashire, where "the sun disappeared, and those lovely blue distances I'd seen on the journey had turned to grey, and rain." [28] As a metaphorical expression more suited to a poet, Helen's health was slowly deteriorating, a sign of things to come in the near future when bright optimism would be replaced by unprecedented despair.

When Helen sent out that slew of typewritten letters to an unknown number of TV producers for the BBC in 1950, she created an avalanche of new opportunities for Peter. "For three years in succession," he recalls, "my work received awards, fulfilling Helen's prediction and her faith in my abilities . . . Whatever success I may have achieved was due entirely to Helen." [29] Yet despite all of her unfailing loyalty and devotion, Peter still experienced manic episodes racked with doubt and depression, but there was always Helen, standing on the sidelines ready to help out in any way possible, most of the time via solid advice and a bit of philosophy. "There is nothing that can defeat a man," she wrote in a letter to Peter, "except his own acceptance of defeat. Of all the men and women I have ever known, you have the greatest courage, integrity, honour, (and) spiritual love . . . Reflect on your victories over the many seemingly insurmountable obstacles—ill-health, poverty, persecution . . . All these you defeated . . . " For an egomaniac, these exceptionally strong words would surely inflate an already bloated self-view, but for Peter, they created comfort and allowed him to consider "How could I fail with such incredible love and support?" [30]

By the late 1960s, Helen's health had deteriorated even further, and her cough, partly due to many years of heavy smoking, worsened to the point where she could not breathe without a steady supply of oxygen. According to her doctor, a specialist in diseases of the pulmonary system, Helen had waited too long for medical treatment for what was now advanced emphysema. "I cannot perform miracles," he stated to Peter, an indication that Helen's condition would not go into remission as it had several times in the past. However, after receiving three weeks of treatments at the "thermal town" of Le Mont-Dore in France, Helen miraculously recovered her health. Her cough "disappeared entirely," says Peter. "She was revitalized, and restored to better health in general." [31]

This rapid improvement in Helen's condition, helped along by the expiration of a lease for a flat and the promise of even better health, created a new sense of balance and optimism in the lives of Helen and Peter Cushing, so much so that they decided to relocate to a "quaint, little fishing town" known as Whitstable, in Kent, not too far from the ancient city of Canterbury and perhaps best-known for its sizable collection of windmills. [32]

One of these structures in Whitstable is known as Black Mill or Borstal Hill Mill. Built in 1815, it was once covered in tar, thus the name of Black Mill. In 1912, a rather well-to-do family with inborn and inbred ties to British theatre was told by former Lyceum actor Frank Tyars that "a property was on the market in the Kentish town of Whitstable," where many theatrical persons owned holiday homes. This was the "Black Windmill with three acres of land and a miller's cottage" standing prominently atop Borstal Hill and looking down into Whitstable, its port, and the North Sea. [33]

In 1928, the youngest son of this family moved into the windmill and quickly converted it into an art studio. This was none other than Laurence Irving, the grandson of Sir Henry Irving and our frequently quoted author of *Henry Irving: The Actor and His World*. As shown by the following thumbnail sketch, Laurence Irving's life shares a number of eerie parallels with that of Peter Cushing. Born in 1897, Irving was an accomplished book illustrator and painter of landscapes and marine settings and spent many years in Hollywood as a set designer and art director. One of the films for which he served as art director was *The Man in the Iron Mask* (1929), starring Douglas Fairbanks and based on Alexander Dumas' novel. In 1930, an exhibition of Irving's watercolors was held at the Fine Arts Society gallery which included "costume and set designs and the originals of his book illustrations." [34] In 1972, at the age of seventy-five, Irving was awarded the OBE (Officer of the Order of the British Empire) by Queen Elizabeth II for his gallant service in the Royal Naval Air Force during World War II. Ironically, Peter Cushing was also seventy-five years old when he was awarded his OBE in March of 1989 by Queen Elizabeth II. [35]

In January 1971, during the very early stages of shooting Hammer's *Blood From the Mummy's Tomb*, Peter was informed by his secretary Joyce Broughton that Helen had been admitted to Canterbury Hospital because of a relapse related to her worsening emphysema. After being told by Helen's doctor that her condition had severely affected her heart, Peter knew that the end was near, despite Helen's "invincible will and courage" and her ability to "overcome bouts of sickness that would have laid low far more robust individuals." [36]

Rather than allow Helen to linger in the hospital, Peter arranged to have her taken home to Whitstable, and so as to tend to her medical needs, he canceled his participation in the Hammer project after a single day of work on the film. [37]

On the morning of Thursday, January 14, 1971, Helen Cushing died from emphysema. "She's gone," said the nurse, and for a long moment, Peter looked down and noticed that all of the signs of Helen's pain and suffering over the last twenty years had faded away. "She looked serenely at peace, and quite beautiful." [38] As would be expected, Peter was utterly devastated by Helen's death, and perhaps for the first time in his adult life felt completely alone, stranded like a lost child in the wilderness of blunt reality. In effect, Peter's supportive net had been pulled from under him. "I felt nothing," he admits, "just empty, my mind as though anaesthetized" [39] and unable to accept the fact that his beloved Helen had passed into the unknown.

In one of the longest poems ever written in the English language, British poetess Elizabeth Barrett Browning describes a certain Aurora Leigh, a headstrong young woman with her own ideas on how to manage her affairs and those of her introverted husband, as a "woman artist who is simultaneously poet and muse," due to inhabiting "the feminine spiritual realm as well as the masculine realm." [40] This is a perfect representation of Helen Cushing, a woman who cherished art and literature and viewed the theatrical stage as a place of wonderment and enchantment. She was also a "muse," a source of great knowledge and inspiration for Peter, much like an ancient Greek goddess that guided the destinies of man for better or for worse. Although Helen did not consider herself as a poet or an artist on a level with her husband, she nevertheless exuded all of the qualities of a visionary, an idealist, a seer, and a dreamer. Helen also realized that life is fleeting and that death may not be the end of all things. As she expresses in her final letter to Peter, "Let the sun shine in your heart. Do not pine for me . . . Do not be hasty to leave this world, because you will not go until you have lived the life you have been given. And remember, we will meet again when the time is right. This is my promise." [41]

§

5

Final
Thoughts

As an actor, Peter Cushing was a great improviser and has long been known for his strict attention to detail, much like a scenic designer who decides what goes where and how a specific scene should be arranged and photographed, the *mise-en-cadre* as contrasted with the *mise-en-scene* or everything that falls within the frame, including actors, set decorations, movement, light and shadow, and especially props, such as a mahogany briar pipe, a magnifying glass, a deerstalker's cap, and a dagger with the Baskerville crest on its hilt, all of the accouterments of Mr. Sherlock Holmes in Hammer's *The Hound of the Baskervilles*, "Props" Peter's first "spell of duty" as the great detective. [1]

Thanks to the interception of Helen who could speak four major languages, Peter became a perfectionist related to his vocal patterns and ways of speaking and forming words when portraying a character. In his autobiography, Peter discusses how he overcame his "slovenly speech and deplorable accent" by "enunciating loudly and repeatedly through contorted mouth" a series of fashionable expressions, such as "The Moon in June is Full of Beauty" (courtesy of Mr. Aynesworth at Guildhall) as an exercise for pronouncing short O's. He also admits that after all of this repetitive practice, "a great deal of polish was required to reach any sort of perfection." [2]

Standing on the sidelines as a sort of vocal mentor was Lewis Cairns James (1865 to 1946), an Edinburgh-born comic baritone and a member of Richard D' Oyly Carte's "B" Opera Company from July 1887 to September 1891. After leaving Mr. Carte's company, James made a career in London and performed at many theatrical venues during the early to mid 1890s like the Royalty, where Wilton Herriot appeared in *Charley's Aunt* in 1892, and the Globe, the theatrical home of William Penley. [3] If Peter knew in the early 1930s that Mr.

James had most likely associated with Herriot and Penley some forty years earlier, he makes no indication of it in his memoirs.

The best way to appreciate Peter's acting eccentricities and mannerisms is to examine one of his personal screenplays (a reading copy) which was sold at auction shortly after his death in 1994 to an unknown bidder and ended up in the hands of yours truly in 1998. Dated May 28, 1980, *The Black Cat*, produced by Selenia Cinematografica of Italy and Klondike Fever Film Productions of Ontario, Canada, and written by Biagio Proietti and Peter Welbeck (*The Face of Fu Manchu*, 1965, and *Vengeance of Fu Manchu*, 1968) with Lucio Fulci as director, is noted as a re-write (i.e., a second draft) and contains numerous notations in Peter's handwriting that uncovers his disciplinary side related to his wardrobe, the shooting schedule for the film, and other details that he considered as crucial to portraying the main protagonist of Robert Miles, a clairvoyant who owns a fiendish feline that stalks the residents of a small English coastal town.

However, Peter did not appear in *The Black Cat* because he pulled out of the project sometime during the spring of 1980, thus opening the door for Patrick Magee, Peter's co-star in *And Now the Screaming Starts* (1973) and *The Skull* (1965), to step in and assume the role of Robert Miles. As a so-called cult classic, *The Black Cat* is mediocre at best, due to its slow, plodding, and weak narrative which is about as frightening as a sober Lon Chaney, Jr., at a Hollywood barbecue. Also, this pseudo-version of Poe's immortal tale about a man driven to madness and murder by a black cat named Pluto, suffers greatly without the presence of Peter Cushing, thus making Fulci's decision to allow him to withdraw from the project ill-conceived and unfortunate.

This screenplay, composed of only those scenes that Peter was suppose to appear in (forty-six in total), contains some very small notes in pencil on the first page—"No cruelty to cats . . . vet must be standing by," a great example of Peter's off-screen persona concerning his feelings on the use of animals on the set. This takes us back to Peter's childhood, circa 1920, when he collected the extremely ephemeral *Puck* and *The Rainbow*, a series of children's comics created by Charles Edward Hamilton that featured the fantastic exploits of Rob the Rover and his amphibian-shaped airplane and a family of animals led by Tiger Tim and his friend Joey the parrot.

Hamilton's preference for anthropomorphic characters seems to be linked to other material written by him long before *Puck* and *The Rainbow*, such as *Sketches of Life and Sport in South Eastern Africa*, published in 1870, and *Oriental Zigzag; Or, Wanderings in Syria, Moab, Abyssinia, and Egypt*, published in 1875. As Peter admits, "I owe (Charles Hamilton) a great debt of gratitude, not only for the enormous pleasure I derived from his work, but also for his influence upon me as a person" [4] in relation to treating animals with respect and admiration.

On the same page, Peter reminds himself to "play Miles oddly, slightly mad to start with," a reference to his intentions to slowly build up the madness of Robert Miles, thus drawing the viewer into the evolving psyche of the character. This approach to character development was used extensively by Peter for many of his film roles in order to create characters with complex personalities like Baron Frankenstein, Dr. Van Helsing, and Osric in Laurence Olivier's 1948 version of *Hamlet*.

On the second to the last page, rendered in blue fountain pen ink, Peter's wardrobe chart notes his preferences for clothing to be worn in his role as Robert Miles. For example, an interior shot of Miles' cellar calls for a two-piece tweed suit (Harris burnt sienna!), a checkered woolen waistcoat, a shirt with a deep collar, a knitted tie, long yellow socks, and a pair of brown shoes or loafers; for an exterior shot of Miles' house, Peter mentions a tweed hat, gloves, and a topcoat (preferably a Macintosh). At the bottom of the chart, a tiny note in pencil says "Hairspray, please."

Peter's shooting schedule occupies the last page of this screenplay and is broken down into various scenes, starting with #4 (INT. MILES' STUDIO. DAY) and ending with #108 (INT. MILES' CELLAR. EVENING). Just below this schedule are the dates of the various shoots, beginning with Monday, August 11 and finishing on Sunday, October 19, a little more than two months in total. Although this provides the exact date when Peter was to begin his role as Robert Miles, the rest of the chart is blank because of his decision to withdraw from the project.

The most fascinating aspect of this screenplay is the additional dialog written by Peter on the back of five creased and soiled, light blue pages taken from another script, possibly *The Man in the Iron Mask*, due to one of the characters, a Mr. Lorry, declaring "Your father. He was left to die in prison but he did not die." Some of Peter's dialog is far superior to that of Proietti and Welbeck which reveals another aspect of Peter's wide-ranging talents as an artist. In one scene with Mimsy Farmer, Peter has altered the dialog to read "You're a lovely girl, Jill. Your hands are gentle and soft, your eyes are clear and deep." Another scene with Peter's own dialog takes us into the dark soul of Robert Miles—"I've never wanted to kill. The beast knows my suppressed hatred and my anger over people's lack of understanding. My frustration became the solitude forced upon me to obey the evil side of my personality, the evil that lives in each of us."

The reason for Peter's decision to withdraw from Fulci's *The Black Cat* is quite simple—the use of gratuitous violence in films did not agree with him, especially if the violence centered around an animal forced to endure strangulation, kicking, or being routinely thrown against a nearby wall. In many ways, Peter exhibited personality traits that can be favorably compared to the unknown narrator in Poe's masterpiece of American literature *The Black Cat*, first published in August of 1843. "From my infancy," declares the narrator, "I was noted for the docility . . . of my disposition. I was especially fond of animals . . . and in my manhood, I derived from it one of my principle sources of pleasure . . . There is something in the unselfish and self-sacrificing love of a brute which goes directly to the heart of him who has had frequent occasion to test the paltry friendship . . . of mere Man." [5]

Over the course of his acting career which began in 1935 and ended in 1983 with the sci-fi romp *Biggles*, Peter worked with a large number of actors and actresses, as well as directors, producers, editors, set designers, technicians, and screenwriters. Besides providing well-grounded opinions on Peter Cushing the man, many of these individuals also offer reminiscences on his amazing talent as an actor and artist. For instance, Peter Vaughn, a co-star in the 1950 play *The Gay Invalid*, notes that Peter was "a meticulous actor (who) worked with great care and precision;" Wolfe Morris, the Sherpa guide in the BBC production *The Creature* (later filmed as *The Abominable Snowman*) notes that Peter possessed an "intellectual grasp of the lines of enquiry" and was a "modern yet truly classical actor;" Peter Graham Scott, director of *Night Creatures*, states that Peter was "an actor of great charm, skill, and intelligence, underrated during his lifetime;"

Kathleen Byron of *Twins of Evil* remarks that Peter was "a most remarkable actor, able to create frightening, evil characters and yet if necessary, portray a warm, caring human being with equal success;" and lastly, Richard Beale, a co-star in the BBC adaptation of *The Caves of Steel*, observes that with Peter, "One always felt the presence of a strange, lost dimension and that he was capable of anything. In my opinion, it was his real self behind the mask that nourished this atmosphere of strangeness and mystery." [6]

Since the great Sir Henry Irving has played such an important role within the pages of *The Unknown Peter Cushing*, we should listen to what he has to say about the art and craft of acting. The following quotes have been taken from "The Art of Acting," an address given by Sir Henry at the Philosophical Institution of Edinburgh, Scotland, on November 9, 1891:

It is the actor's part to represent or interpret the ideas and emotions which the poet has created, and to do this, he must have a full knowledge and understanding of them. This in itself is no easy task, for it requires much study and labour of many kinds. Having then acquired an idea, the actor's intention to work it out into reality. Now and again, it suffices the poet to think and write in abstractions, but the actor's work is absolutely concrete. [7]

Toward the end of his address, Sir Henry makes it abundantly clear that the ultimate aim of acting is to reproduce beauty:

Truth itself is only an element of acting, and to merely reproduce things vile and squalid and mean is a debasement of art. Life, with all its pains and sorrows, is a beautiful and precious gift, and the actor's role is to reproduce this beautiful thing. And thus, every actor who is more than a mere machine, and who has an ideal of any kind, has a duty that lies beyond the scope of his personal ambition. His art must be something to hold in reverence if he wishes others to hold it in esteem. [8]

Of all the individuals that intimately knew Peter Cushing during his lifetime, one stands out in particular, a man whom Peter often referred to as his best and dearest friend, perhaps the male equivalent to Helen as a source of inspiration and guidance. This would be Peter

Gray, once employed by Sir Basil Blackwell, the proprietor of Blackwell booksellers which opened to the public in 1897 and published a number of books by prominent British authors like poet W.H. Auden (whose older brother opted for the life of a farmer), and J.R.R. Tolkien of *The Lord of the Rings* trilogy.

According to Peter Cushing, his mother was very fond of Mr. Gray and was elated to know that her son had a boon companion, "a real chum, a real pal and friend." [9] Luckily, Peter Gray agreed to write the foreword to *Past Forgetting: Memoirs of the Hammer Years* which offers first-person observations on Peter's talent as an actor and gives us a more clear idea of what actor Richard Beale refers to as a "strange, lost dimension," an "atmosphere of strangeness and mystery":

Make-believe, that childhood propensity, had more attraction for than reality, and it was this total suspension of disbelief in the far-fetched phantasies of his horror films that enabled him to make the incredible credible. In an indefinable way, I believe that his freshness of vision, his seeing of the commonplace as if for the first time always, adds an extra dimension, a touch of the marvelous, to everything he does as a player, and accounts in part for his worldwide appeal. [10]

****

As mentioned in the introduction, it is not clear how much Peter Cushing actually knew concerning the theatrical career of his grandfather Henry William Cushing. All we really have to go on is what he included in his 1986 autobiography. But without a doubt, Peter knew absolutely nothing about John Cushing the actor, due to his obscurity and the lack of readily available books and other documents that provide even a glimpse into his life as an eighteenth century stage performer. How I wish it was possible to travel back in time to the Famous Monsters Convention of 1975 in New York City (Peter's only personal appearance at a film convention as far as I have been able to determine) and present him with a copy of *The Unknown Peter Cushing*. I have often wondered how he might react to it, perhaps with astonishment, or bewilderment, or perhaps with something as simple as a raised eyebrow and a devious grin.

In spite of all my efforts as a researcher, certain areas of Peter Cushing's life shall remain unknown, at least until someone takes it upon himself to write a full-blown biography, similar to Christopher Gullo's *In All Sincerity* but more in-depth and with additional coverage on Peter's personal life outside of the influence of Helen. What I would truly like to see is for some hardy and brave soul to make the decision to travel to England (unless you already call England your home) and start digging in places like the British Library and its massive newspaper collection, the Victoria and Albert Museum, the Library and Museum of Freemasonry, and other archives dedicated to the theatrical arts and the performers that made British theatre in the eighteenth, nineteenth and twentieth centuries possible. To be truly honest, my mind boggles at the possibilities regarding what might be found and what it possibly might reveal. But if you do decide to start digging, please remember the words of the great Oscar Wilde—"Those who go beneath the surface do so at their own peril."

§

Endnotes

INTRODUCTION

1. *An Autobiography* (London: Weidenfeld & Nicolson, 1986), 143.

2. Letter dated August 18, 2001 (author's collection).

3. *Lord of Misrule: The Autobiography of Christopher Lee* (London: Orion, 2003), 298.

4. Christopher Gullo, *In All Sincerity . . . Peter Cushing* (Xlibris, 2004), 115.

5. *Autobiography*, 5.

6. Ibid, 10.

7. Ibid, 10.

8. Ibid, 10.

9. Ibid, 38.

10. Ibid, 10.

11. Ibid, 12.

12. Ibid, 12.

13. Ibid, 142.

14. Ibid, 30.

ROGUES, VAGABONDS, AND SCOUNDRELS

1. J. Raithby, ed. *Statutes at Large*, Vol. 5 (London: Eyre & Strahan, 1811), 266-268.

2. Ibid, 268.

3. Cushing Genealogy: British and European Ancestors, RootsWeb, 2005.

4. *An Account of the Ancestors and Descendants of Matthew Cushing Who Came to America in 1638.* Re-issued by James Cushing, the Perrault Printing Company, Montreal, Canada, 1905.

5. Ibid.

6. Ibid.

7. David Cushing, Genealogy of the Cushing Family, Internet, 2010.

8. Ibid.

9. *Lives of the Poets* (London: Oxford UP, 1946), 176.

10. Desmond Shawe-Taylor, *Covent Garden* (London: Max Parrish, 1948), 9.

11. Ibid, 11.

12. Martha Fletcher Bellinger, *A Short History of the Theatre* (NY: Henry Holt & Company, 1927), 249. Quoting James Branch Cabell.

13. Philip H. Highfill, et al. *A Biographical Dictionary of Actors, Actresses, Musicians, Dancers, Managers and Other Stage Personnel in London, 1660-1800*, Vol. 4: Corye to Dynion (Carbondale: Southern Illinois UP, 1973), 101.

14. *Eminent Actors: Charles Macklin* (Kegan Paul, Trench & Trubner, 1890), 52.

15. Ibid, 52.

16. Arthur Hornblow, The Coming of the Hallams, Internet, 2005.

17. Christopher Gullo, *In All Sincerity . . . Peter Cushing* (Xlibris, 2004), 62.

18. Highfill, *A Biographical Dictionary*, 101-102.

19. Raymond Mander, *The Theatres of London* (London: New English Library, Barnard's Inn, 1975), 88.

20. *A Biographical Dictionary*, 102.

21. (London: Chatto & Windus, 1880), 338.

22. Highfill, *A Biographical Dictionary*, 103.

23. Jessica Byrd, commentator. *The Busie Body*, by Susanna Centlivre. Project Gutenberg, September 24, 2005.

24. Highfill, *A Biographical Dictionary*, 103. All of John Cushing's children were born after 1751, thus making it obvious that he remarried after Mary Cushing's death.

25. *Wandsworth Past* (London: Historical Publications, Ltd., 1998), 26.

26. W. Clark Russell, *Representative Actors* (London: Frederick Warne, 1883), 50.

27. Ibid, 71.

28. Ibid, 215.

29. Bodlein Library, University of Oxford, Internet, 2010.

THE LIFE AND TIMES OF HENRY WILLIAM CUSHING

1. James Huneker, *Iconoclasts: A Book of Dramatists* (NY: Charles Scribner's Sons, 1905), 157.

2. Paula G. Sitarz, *The Curtain Rises: A History of European Theatre from the Eighteenth Century to the Present* (Cincinnati, OH: Betterway Books, 1993), 63.

3. Ibid, 63.

4. *Henry Irving: The Actor and His World*, 42 & 44.

5. Ibid, 44-45.

6. Ibid, 33.

7. Madeleine Bingham, *Henry Irving: The Greatest Victorian Actor* (NY: Stein & Day, 1978), 20-21.

8. Christopher Hibbert, ed. *The London Encyclopedia* (UK: Macmillan, 2001), 356.

9. Family Search International Genealogical Index, v.5.0. RootsWeb, Internet, 2009.

10. *Victorian England* (NY: Greenhaven Press, 2000), 186.

11. Norfolk Family History Society, Internet, 2010.

12. *The Stage*, January 27, 1897, p. 13.

13. Kristi McNultry, assistant librarian for local history, Fremantle City Library, Fremantle, Western Australia, November 2010.

14. *Autobiography*, 13.

15. Dorian Gerhold, *Wandsworth Past* (London: Historical Publications, Ltd., 1998), 37.

16. Ibid, 71-74.

17. David Stuckey, *Card Times: The Cushing Collection* (UK: Magpie Publications & the Peter Cushing Estate, 1999), 19.

18. *Autobiography*, 10.

19. November 2, 1905, p. 3.

20. *The London Building World of the 1860's* (London: Thames & Hudson, 1973), 34.

21. October 31, 1875, issue 1936.

22. January 20, 1878, issue 2052.

23. Master and Margarita: Gounod's *Faust*. Adapted from Quaintance Eaton's *Opera: A Pictorial Guide* (NY: Abaris, 1980), Internet, 2005.

24. February 3, 1878, issue 2054.

25. February 6, 1878. p. 9, issue 29171, col. A.

26. David Ewen, ed. *The Complete Book of Classical Music* (Englewood Cliffs, NJ: Prentice-Hall, 1965), 163.

27. *The Mapleson Memoirs: The Career of an Operatic Impressario, 1858-1888*. ed. Harold Rosenthal (NY: Appleton-Century, 1966), 107-108.

28. September 29, 1883, issue 2349.

29. February 16, 1884, issue 2369.

30. Ibid, 118.

31. Page 12, col. 4.

32. *The Mapleson Memoirs*, 313.

33. April 2, 1887, issue 2532.

34. *The Life of Sir Arthur Conan Doyle* (NY: Harper & Row, 1949), 49-50.

35. H. Rider Haggard's *She*, Internet, 1967.

36. Hugh Walker, *The Literature of the Victorian Era* (Cambridge UP, 1931), 810.
37. Laurence Irving, *Henry Irving*, 493.
38. The Whitechapel Murder, September 14, 1888, p. 4, issue 32491, col. F.
39. *The Era*, March 23, 1889, issue 2635.
40. *The Stage*, October 26, 1883, p. 12.
41. Ibid, August 1, 1884, p. 12.
42. Ibid, September 3, 1886, p. 12.
43. November 11, 1887, p. 17.
44. *The Stage*, July 12, 1889, p. 9.
45. Obituary: Mr. W.S. Penley, p. 13, issue 40054, col. B.
46. *Autobiography*, 12.
47. Ibid.
48. Lodge of Asaph, *The Era*, November 7, 1885, issue 2459.
49. Members or Masons: One-Day Classes and the Initiatic Tradition. Internet, 2003.
50. Ray Dotson, Masonic Poetry through the Ages, Internet, 2010. "Inscription on a large medal struck in December, 1838 in response to an interdict against the Masonic Order by the Roman Catholic Archbishop of Mechlin. Around the border is inscribed a Latin phrase meaning "Masonry will Live, God wills it. Grand Orient of Belgium, 5838."
51. Ibid.
52. *William Terriss and Richard Prince: Two Players in an Adelphi Melodrama* (London: Society for Theatre Research, 1987), 55.
53. *The Era*, November 7, 1885, issue 2459.
54. *The Era*, November 6, 1886, issue 2511.
55. *The Era*, November 9, 1889, issue 2668.
56. George Rowell, *William Terriss and Richard Prince*, 56.
57. Andrew Prescott, Brother Irving: Sir Henry Irving and Freemasonry, The Irving Society, Internet, 2003.
58. Ibid.
59. Hugh Walker, *The Literature of the Victorian Era*, 1050.
60. Vyvyan Holland, intro. *The Complete Works of Oscar Wilde* (NY: Harper Collins, 1989), 11.
61. *Henry Irving: The Greatest Victorian Actor*, 121.
62. *From the Bells to King Arthur* (London: John MacQueen, 1896), 115-116.
63. *Victorian Actors and Actresses in Review* (Westport, CT: Greenwood Press, 1983), xix.
64. *The Stage*, July 2, 1891, p. 8.
65. Madeleine Bingham, *Henry Irving*, 561.
66. *The Stage*, May 5, 1892, p. 11.
67. *The Era*, April 9, 1892, issue 2794.
68. Laurence Irving, *Henry Irving*, 561.

69. Ibid, 562.

70. Ibid, 562.

71. *The Era*, July 15, 1893, issue 2860.

72. Laurence Irving, *Henry Irving*, 467.

73. *The Life of Henry Irving*, Vol. II. (London: Longmans, Green & Company, 1908), 92.

74. Tom Prideaux, *Love or Nothing: The Life and Times of Ellen Terry* (NY: Charles Scribner's Sons, 1975), 167.

75. *Victorian Actors and Actresses in Review*, xix.

76. Laurence Irving, *Henry Irving*, 452.

77. *Henry Irving* (London: J.M. Dent & Sons, Ltd.), 111.

78. Sylvia Starshine, *Dracula, or The Undead: A Play in Prologue and Five Acts by Bram Stoker* (Nottingham, UK: Pumpkin Books, 1997).

79. *Henry Irving: A Record and Review* (London: George Bell & Sons, 1899), 223.

80. *The Era*, June 8, 1895, issue 2959.

81. Laurence Irving, *Henry Irving*, 581.

82. *The Era*, September 21, 1985, issue 2974.

83. March 26, 1891, p. 8.

84. *The Era*, November 9, 1895, issue 2981.

85. Laurence Irving, *Henry Irving*, 597.

86. *The Era*, November 7, 1896, issue 3033.

87. Ibid.

88. Ibid.

89. Sylvia Starshine, *Dracula, or The Undead*, xii.

90. *Bram Stoker: A Biography of the Author of Dracula* (NY: Knopf, 1996), 270.

91. Amy Wong, "Marryat's The Blood of the Vampire: A Forgotten Vampire Story." Internet, 2010.

92. History: The Murder of William Terriss, Actor's Benevolent Fund, Internet, 2010.

93. *The Era*, December, 1897, issue 3065.

94. *Henry Irving*, 613.

95. William Archer, *The Theatrical World of 1897* (NY: Benjamin Blom, 1969, rpt. 1898 ed.), 385, 393 & 399.

96. *British Plays of the Nineteenth Century* (NY: The Odyssey Press, 1966), 9.

97. *Henry Irving*, 618-619.

98. Walter Jerrod, ed. *The Complete Poetical Works of Thomas Hood* (London: Oxford UP, 1935), 135.

99. Pg. 12, col. 4.

100. Ibid.

101. *Autobiography*, 12.

102. Laurence Irving, *Henry Irving*, 628.

103. *Victorian Actors and Actresses in Review*, xxvii.

104. *In All Sincerity . . . Peter Cushing* (Xlibris, 2004), 20.

THE MOON IN JUNE IS FULL OF BEAUTY

1. *Studio and Stage* (NY: Benjamin Blom, Inc., 1972), 276.

2. *Henry Irving* (London: J.M. Dent & Sons, Ltd., 1930), 78.

3. The First Years. Equity Timeline, Internet, 2006.

4. David Duffey, The D'Oyly Carte Family, Gilbert & Sullivan Archive, Internet, 2003.

5. From a painting owned by Cushing collector Dan Dorman.

6. *Autobiography*, 17-18.

7. Dime Novels and Penny Dreadfuls, Stanford University Dime Novel and Story Paper Collection, Internet, 2011.

8. Peter Cushing Video Newsreel Film, Internet, 2010.

9. *Autobiography*, 19-20.

10. George Speaight, *Punch and Judy: A History* (London: Studio Vista, Ltd., 1970), 36.

11. *An Autobiography*, 35.

12. Ibid, 35.

13. Ibid, 36-37.

14. Ibid, 11-12.

15. Ibid, 37-38.

16. Golden Fleece Lodge, Internet, 2011.

17. *Autobiography*, 42.

18. Ibid, 43.

19. Ibid, 44.

20. Ibid, 45.

21. Ibid, 47.

22. Ibid, 48.

23. Ibid, 49.

24. Ibid, 49-50.

25. Ibid, 50-51.

26. Ibid, 51.

27. George B. Bryan, Comp. *Stage Deaths: A Biographical Guide to International Theatrical Obituaries, 1850 to 1990* (Westport, CT: Greenwood Press, 1991), 257.

28. *Autobiography*, 53.

29. Ibid, 53.

30. 10 & 13.

31. Ibid, 56.

32. Summer, 2002, In Christopher Gullo, *In All Sincerity . . . Peter Cushing* (Xlibris, 2004), 29.

33. Doreen Hawkins, *Drury Lane to Dimapur: Wartime Adventures of an Actress* (UK: Dovecote Press, 2009, 23.

34. *Autobiography*, 57.

35. Alan Chudley, Hasting's Theatres and Halls, Internet, n.d.

36. July 14, 1938. p. 7.

37. August 25, 1938, p. 10.

38. *The Stage*, July 14 & August 25, 1938, pgs. 7 & 10.

39. *Autobiography*, 59-60.

40. Ibid, 60.

41. Obituary—Walter Larney Goodkind, NYT Archives, Internet, 2003.

42. *Autobiography*, 63.

43. Gregory William Mank, *It's Alive! The Classic Cinema Saga of Frankenstein* (NY: A.S. Barnes, 1981), 15.

44. Ibid, 16.

45. Sheridan Morely, *Brits in Hollywood: Tales from the Hollywood Raj* (UK: Robson Books, 2006), 9-10.

46. *Autobiography*, 78.

47. Ibid, 80.

HELEN: THE POETRY OF HER PRESENCE

1. *Edgar Allan Poe: A Critical Biography* (NY: Appleton-Century-Crofts, 1941), 86.

2. Ibid, 86.

3. *The Poe Reader* (Ann Arbor, MI: State Street Press, 1996), 520.

4. 84-85.

5. *Autobiography*, 86.

6. Ibid, 86-87.

7. RootsWeb, Internet, 2010.

8. Ibid.

9. Finnish Literature Society, Helsinki, Finland, Internet, n.d.

10. RootsWeb, Internet, 2010.

11. *Autobiography*, 92.

12. Ibid, 90-91.

13. Ibid, 92.

14. Ibid, 92.

15. September 27, 1945, p. 5.

16. Gerald Eades Bentley, *The Jacobean and Caroline Stage*, Vol. II (Oxford, UK: Clarendon Press, 1941), 448.

17. November 28, 1946, p. 4.

18. *Autobiography*, 102.

19. Ibid, 108.

20. January 27, 1948, p. 7.

21. February 3, 1949, p. 7.

22. May 3, 1956, p. 9.

23. August 13, 1959, p. 18.

24. *Autobiography*, 111.

25. Ibid, 113-114.

26. December 4, 1958, p. 14.

27. Edward Seago, 1910-1974, Internet, 2011.

28. *Autobiography*, 115.

29. Ibid, 119.

30. Ibid, 123-124.

31. Ibid, 129-130.

32. Ibid, 130.

33. Laurence Irving, *Designing for the Movies: The Memoirs of Laurence Irving* (Lanham, MD: Scarecrow Press, 2005), xiii. Published posthumously.

34. Ibid, xviii.

35. Ibid, 224.

36. *An Autobiography*, 139.

37. Christopher Gullo, *In All Sincerity . . . Peter Cushing* (Xlibris, 2004), 213.

38. *An Autobiography*, 141.

39. Ibid, 141.

40. Joyce Zonana, The Embodied Muse: Elizabeth Barrett Browning's *Aurora Leigh* and Feminist Poetics, *Tulsa Studies in Women's Literature* 2 (1989): 243.

41. *An Autobiography*, 143.

FINAL THOUGHTS

1. Peter Cushing, *Past Forgetting: Memoirs of the Hammer Years* (London: Weidenfeld & Nicolson, 1988), 78.

2. (London: Weidenfeld & Nicolson, 1986), 50-51.

3. Who Was Who in The D'Oyly Carte Opera Company, Internet, 2011.

4. *Autobiography*, 18.

5. *The Poe Reader* (Ann Arbor, MI: State Street Press, 1996), 3-4.

6. Christopher Gullo, *In All Sincerity . . . Peter Cushing* (Xlibris, 2004), 67, 103, 157, 216, 171.

7. Laurence Irving, *Henry Irving: The Actor and His World* (NY: Macmillan, 1952), 680.

8. Ibid, 684.

9. *Past Forgetting: Memoirs of the Hammer Years*, 38.

10. Ibid, 14-15.

§

Bibliography

Archer, William, ed. *Eminent Actors: Charles Macklin*. London: Kegan Paul, Trench, & Trubner, 1890.

—. *The Theatrical World of 1897*. New York: Benjamin Blom, 1969 (Rpt. 1898 ed.).

Bailey, J. O. *British Plays of the Nineteenth Century: An Anthology to Illustrate the Evolution of the Drama*. New York: Odyssey Press, Inc., 1966.

Belford, Barbara. *Bram Stoker: A Biography of the Author of Dracula*. New York: Alfred A. Knopf, 1996.

Bellinger, Martha Fletcher. *A Short History of the Theatre*. New York: Henry Holt & Company, 1927.

Bentley, Gerald Eades. *The Jacobean and Caroline Stage: Dramatic Companies and Players*. Oxford, UK: Clarendon Press, 1941.

Bingham, Madeleine. *Henry Irving: The Greatest Victorian Actor*. New York: Stein & Day, 1978.

Brereton, Austin. *The Life of Henry Irving*. Vol. II. London: Longmans, Green & Company, 1908.

Bryan, George B., Comp. *Stage Deaths: A Biographical Guide to International Theatrical Obituaries, 1850 to 1990*. Westport, CT: Greenwood Press, 1991.

Byrd, Jessica, commentator. "The Busie Body, by Susanna Centlivre." September 24, 2005. http://www.gutenberg.org/files/16740/16740-8.txt.

Carr, John Dickson. *The Life of Sir Arthur Conan Doyle*. New York: Harper & Row, 1949.

Chambers, E.K. *The Elizabethan Stage*. Vol. III. Oxford: Clarendon Press, 1923.

Chornenky, Dennis V. "Members or Masons: One-Day Classes and the Initiatic Tradition." 2003. http://www.masonicrestoration.com/images/ DVC_Members_Or_Masons .pdf.

Chudley, Alan. "Hastings Theatres and Halls." n.d. http://www.arthurlloyd.co.uk/ Hastings.htm.

Churchill, Sir Winston. *History of the English-Speaking Peoples*. New York: Dodd, Mead & Company, 1965.

Cooper, Barbara T., Ed. *Dictionary of Literary Biography*. Vol. 192—French Dramatists, 1789-1914. University of New Hampshire, The Gale Group, 1998.

Craig, Edward Gordon. *Henry Irving*. London: J.M. Dent & Sons, 1930.

Cushing, David. "Genealogy of the Cushing Family." 2010. http://freepages.genealogy. rootsweb.ancestry.com/~cushing.

Cushing, Lemuel. *The Genealogy of the Cushing Family*. Montreal, Canada: Lovell Printing and Publishing Company, 1877.

Cushing, Peter. *Peter Cushing: An Autobiography*. London: Weidenfeld & Nicolson, 1986.

—. *Past Forgetting: Memoirs of the Hammer Years*. London: Weidenfeld & Nicolson, 1988.

Bibliography

Cushing, Warren R. "Cushing Genealogy: British & European Ancestors." 2005. http://worldconnect.genealogy.rootsweb.com/cgi-bin/igm.cgi?op=GET&db=wrcushing1&id=1588107491.

Del Vecchio, Deborah and Tom Johnson. *Peter Cushing: The Gentle Man of Horror and His 91 Films*. Jefferson, NC: McFarland & Company, 1992.

"Dime Novels and Penny Dreadfuls." Stanford University Dime Novel and Story Paper Collection. 2011. http://library.stanford.edu/depts/dp/pennies/home.html.

Dotson, Ray. "Masonic Poetry through the Ages." 2010. http://www.masonicsites.org/ blue/masonicpoetry.html.

Duffey, David. "The D'Oyly Carte Family." The Gilbert & Sullivan Archive. 2003. http://math.boisestate.edu/gas/html/carte.html.

"Early Days." Actors Benevolent Fund. 2010. http://www.actorsbenevolentfund.co.uk/page.asp?id=history2.

"Edward Seago, 1910-1974." 2011. http://www.richard-green.com/DesktopDefault. aspx?tabid=45&tabindex=44&artistid=832.

"Equity at a Glance." Actors' Equity Association. 2010. http://www.actorsequity.org/docs/about/equity_glance.pdf.

Ewen, David, Ed. *The Complete Book of Classical Music*. Englewood Cliffs, NJ: Prentice-Hall, 1965.

"Florence Marryat." The D'Oyly Carte Opera Company. 2001. http://math.boisestate.edu/gas/whowaswho/M/MarryatFlorence.htm.

Gerhold, Dorian. *Wandsworth Past*. London: Historical Publications, Ltd., 1998.

Golden Fleece Lodge. 2011. www.4739.org.uk.

Harker, Joseph. *Studio and Stage*. New York: Benjamin Blom, 1972 (rpt. London, 1924).

Hawkins, Doreen. *Drury Lane to Dimapur: Wartime Adventures of an Actress*. UK: Dovecote Press, 2009.

"Her Majesty's Theatre." *London Times*. Wednesday, February 6, 1878. pg. 9, issue 29171, col. A.

Hiatt, Charles. *Henry Irving: A Record and Review*. London: George Bell & Sons, 1899.

Hibbert, Christopher, Ed. *The London Encyclopedia*. UK: Macmillan, 2001.

Highfill, Philip H., Jr., Kalman A. Burnim & Edward A. Langhans. *A Biographical Dictionary of Actors, Actresses, Musicians, Dancers, Managers and Other Stage Personnel in London, 1660-1800*. Vol. 4: Corye to Dynion. Carbondale: Southern Illinois University Press, 1973.

"History: The Murder of William Terriss." 2011. http://www2.actorsbenevolentfund. co.uk/history-3.html.

Holland, Vyvyan. *The Complete Works of Oscar Wilde*. New York: Harper Collins, 1989.

Hopwood, Jon C. "Biography of John Martin Harvey." 2011. www.imdb.com.

Hornblow, Arthur. "The Coming of the Hallams." A History of the Theatre in America. Vol. 1. Philadelphia: J.B. Lippincott & Company, 1919, pps. 66-87. 2011. http://www. theatrehistory.com/american/hornblow03.html.

Irving, Laurence. *Henry Irving: The Actor and His World*. New York: Macmillan, 1952.

—. *Designing for the Movies: The Memoirs of Laurence Irving*. Lanham, MD: Scarecrow Press, 2005.

Jerrod, Walter, ed. *The Complete Poetical Works of Thomas Hood*. London: Oxford University Press, 1935.

Johnson, Samuel. *Lives of the Poets*. London: Oxford University Press, 1946.

Keating, Rian. "William Terriss." 2011. http://www.ellenterry.org./williamterriss.htm.

Lee, Christopher. *Lord of Misrule: The Autobiography of Christopher Lee*. London: Orion Books, Ltd., 2003.

Leerssen, Jospeh. *Mere Irish and Fior-Ghael: Studies in Irish Nationality, Its Development and Literary Expression Prior to the 19th Century*. Ph.D. diss. Utrecht, 1986.

Litman, Jessica. "The Invention of Common Law Play Right." 2010. http://www-personal.umich.edu/~jdlitman/papers/PlayRight.pdf.

"Lodge of Asaph." *The Era*. Saturday, November 7, 1885, issue 2459. The British Library, 19th Century British Library Newspapers.

London Times. Classified Advertisements on "Her Majesty's Theatre" (Gounod's *Faust*), Thursday, February 7, 1878. pg. 8, Issue 29172, col. C; "Verdi's opera *La Traviata*." Wednesday, October 17, 1883. pg. 1, issue 30953, col. A.

Mander, Raymond. *The Theatres of London*. London: New English Library, Barnard's Inn, 1975.

Mank, Gregory William. *It's Alive! The Classic Cinema Saga of Frankenstein*. La Jolla, CA: A.S. Barnes & Company, 1981.

Mapleson, James Henry. *The Mapleson Memoirs: The Career of an Operatic Impressario, 1858-1888*. Ed. Harold Rosenthal. New York: Appleton-Century, 1966.

"Master and Margarita: Gounod's *Faust*. Adapted from Quaintance Eaton's *Opera: A Pictorial Guide*." (NY: Abaris, 1980). 2011. http://cr.middlebury.edu/public/russian/Bulgakov/public_html/Gounod.html.

Morley, Henry. *Memoirs of Bartholomew Fair*. London: Chatto & Windus, 1880.

Morely, Sheridan. *Brits in Hollywood: Tales from the Hollywood Raj*. UK: Robson Books, Ltd., 2006.

Mullin, Donald, Comp. & Ed. *Victorian Actors and Actresses in Review: A Dictionary of Contemporary Views of Representative British and American Actors and Actresses, 1837-1901*. Westport, CT: Greenwood Press, 1983.

Nadel, Ira B., Ed. *Dictionary of Literary Biography*. Vol. 21. Victorian Novelists Before 1885. University of British Columbia, The Gale Group, 1983.

Norfolk Family History Society. 2010. http://www.norfolkfhs.org.uk/indexes/transcripts. asp.

"Obituary—Mr. W.S. Penley." *London Times*. Tuesday, November 12, 1912. pg. 13, issue 40054, col. B.

"Obituary—Walter Larney Goodkind." New York Times Archive. March 11, 2003. http://www.nytimes.com/2003/03/11/classified/paid-notice-deaths-goodkind-walter-larney.html.

Pascoe, Charles E. *The Dramatic List: A Record Of Principal Performers of Living Actors and Actresses of the British Stage with Criticism from Contemporary Journals*. London: Hardwicke & Bogue, 1879.

—. *Dramatic Notes: A Chronicle of the London Stage, 1879-1882*. London: David Bogue, 1883.

"Peter Cushing Video Newsreel Film." 2010. http://www.britishpathe.com/record. php?id=639.

Poe, Edgar Allan. *The Poe Reader*. Ann Arbor, MI: State Street Press, 1996.

Prescott, Andrew. "Brother Irving: Sir Henry Irving and Freemasonry." 2003. http://www. theirvingsociety.org.uk/brother_irving.htm.

Prideaux, Tom. *Love or Nothing: The Life and Times of Ellen Terry*. New York: Charles Scribner's Sons, 1975.

Raithby, J. Ed. *Statutes at Large*. Vol. 5. London: Eyre & Strahan, 1811.

Reaney, P.H. *A Dictionary of British Surnames*. London: Routledge & Kegan Paul, 1966.

Rowell, George, Ed. *Nineteenth Century Plays*. London: Oxford University Press, 1953.

—. *The Victorian Theatre*. London: Oxford University Press, 1956.

—. *Victorian Dramatic Criticism*. London: Methuen & Company, Ltd., 1971.

—. *William Terriss and Richard Prince: Two Players in an Adelphi Melodrama*. London: Society for Theatre Research, 1987.

Russell, W. Clark. *Representative Actors: A Collection of Criticisms, Anecdotes, Personal Descriptions, Referring to Many Celebrated British Actors from the Sixteenth to the Present Century*. London: Frederick Warne & Company, 1883.

Scott, Clement. *Thirty Years at the Play*. London: The Railway and General Automatic Library, Ltd., 1890.

—. *From 'The Bells' to 'King Arthur': A Critical Record of the First Night Productions at the Lyceum Theatre from 1871 to 1895*. London: John McQueen, 1896.

Shaw, George Bernard. *Our Theatres in the Nineties*. Vol. 3. London: Constable, 1932.

Shawe-Taylor, Desmond. *Covent Garden*. London: Max Parrish & Company, Ltd., 1948.

Sitarz, Paula G. *The Curtain Rises: A History of European Theatre from the Eighteenth Century to the Present*. Vol. II. Cincinnati, OH: Betterway Books, 1993.

Speaight, George. *Punch and Judy: A History*. London: Studio Vista, Ltd., 1970.

Starshine, Sylvia. *Dracula, or, the Undead: A Play in Prologue and Five Acts*. Nottingham, UK: Pumpkin Books, 1997.

Stephen, Leslie and Sidney Lee. *The Dictionary of National Biography*. London: Smith, Elder, 1885-1901.

Stoker, Bram. *Personal Reminiscences of Henry Irving*. 1st American ed. 2 Vols. New York: Macmillan, 1906.

Stuckey, David, Comp. *Card Times: The Cushing Collection*. UK: Magpie Publications & the Peter Cushing Estate, 1999.

Summerson, John. *The London Building World of the Eighteen Sixties*. London: Thames & Hudson, 1973.

Swisher, Clarice. *Victorian England*. New York: Greenhaven Press, 2000.

The British Library. Seventeenth and Eighteenth Century Burney Collection of Newspapers. April 22, 2008. http://find.galegroup.com/bncn.

"The First Years." 2006. http://www.actorsequity.org/aboutequity/timeline/timeline_firstyears.html.

The John Johnson Collection of Printed Ephemera. Bodlein Library, University of Oxford. 2010. http://www.bodley.ox.ac.uk/johnson.

The Library and Museum of Freemasonry. 2010. www.freemasonry.london.museum.

"The Murders in London." *London Times*. October 20, 1888. pg. 7, issue 32522, col. G.

The Official J.B. Priestley Website. 2011. http://www.jbpriestley.co.uk/JBP/Home.html.

"The Whitechapel Murder." *London Times*. September 14, 1888. pg. 4, issue 32491, col. F.
Walker, Hugh. *The Literature of the Victorian Era*. UK: Cambridge University Press, 1931.

Ward, A.W., Ed. *The Cambridge History of English and American Literature*. Vol. 8. New York: G.P. Putnam's Sons, 1907-21.

Wearing, J. Peter. *The London Stage, 1890-1899: A Calendar of Plays and Players*. 2 Vols. Metuchen, NJ: Scarecrow Press, 1976.

White, Eric Walter. *A History of English Opera*. London: Faber, 1983.

"Who Was Who in the D'Oyly Carte Opera Company." 2011. http://webcache.googleusercontent.com/search?q=cache:http://math.boisestate.edu/gas/whowaswho/index.htm

Wilson, A. E. *The Lyceum*. London: Dennis Yates, 1952.

Wollheim, Donald A. "H. Rider Haggard's *She*." 1967. http://www.violetbooks.com/don-wollheim.html.

BIBLIOGRAPHY

Wong, Amy. "Marryat's *The Blood of the Vampire*: A Forgotten Vampire Story."
2010. http://www.suite101.com/content/marryats-the-blood-of-the-vampire-a-forgotten-vampire-story-a259567.

Zonana, Joyce. "The Embodied Muse: Elizabeth Barrett Browning's *Aurora Leigh* and Feminist Poetics." *Tulsa Studies in Women's Literature* 2 (1989): 241-62.

§

Index

Lightning Source UK Ltd.
Milton Keynes UK
UKOW031930300513

211532UK00013B/713/P

9 781593 936655